The Macat Library
世界思想宝库钥匙丛书

解析亚里士多德
《政治学》

AN ANALYSIS OF
ARISTOTLE'S
POLITICS

Katherine Berrisford　Riley Quinn ◎ 著
杨　乐 ◎ 译

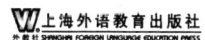

目 录

引言 1
    亚里士多德其人 2
    《政治学》的主要内容 3
    《政治学》的学术价值 4

第一部分：学术渊源 7
    1. 作者生平与历史背景 8
    2. 学术背景 12
    3. 主导命题 16
    4. 作者贡献 20

第二部分：学术思想 25
    5. 思想主脉 26
    6. 思想支脉 30
    7. 历史成就 34
    8. 著作地位 38

第三部分：学术影响 43
    9. 最初反响 44
    10. 后续争议 48
    11. 当代印迹 52
    12. 未来展望 56

术语表 60
人名表 64

CONTENTS

WAYS IN TO THE TEXT 71
   Who Was Aristotle? 72
   What Does *Politics* Say? 73
   Why Does *Politics* Matter? 75

SECTION 1: INFLUENCES 79
   Module 1: The Author and the Historical Context 80
   Module 2: Academic Context 85
   Module 3: The Problem 90
   Module 4: The Author's Contribution 94

SECTION 2: IDEAS 99
   Module 5: Main Ideas 100
   Module 6: Secondary Ideas 105
   Module 7: Achievement 110
   Module 8: Place in the Author's Work 114

SECTION 3: IMPACT 119
   Module 9: The First Responses 120
   Module 10: The Evolving Debate 125
   Module 11: Impact and Influence Today 129
   Module 12: Where Next? 134

Glossary of Terms 138
People Mentioned in the Text 143
Works Cited 147

引言

要 点

- 亚里士多德（公元前384—322年）是一位古希腊哲学家。
- 其著作《政治学》据称写于公元前335—323年。亚里士多德在书中提出，政治共同体为人类的繁荣提供了必要条件。
- 亚里士多德的思想至今仍有说服力。

亚里士多德其人

《政治学》的作者亚里士多德是一位哲学家，公元前384年生于希腊半岛东北部马其顿王国斯塔吉拉城，17岁时前往古希腊学术中心雅典，师从哲学家柏拉图*，后者被许多人视为西方最伟大的思想家。亚里士多德一直求学于柏拉图学园*，直至公元前348年。

公元前343年，亚里士多德重返马其顿王国，成为青年亚历山大大帝*的私人导师，亚历山大后来征服了包括希腊在内的地中海沿岸国家以及欧亚、北非的大片领土。

这些年间，希腊的政治结构发生了巨大变化。几个世纪以来，由小型城邦及其周边领土构成的城邦制*主导了希腊的政治生活。但马其顿统治者已开始缔造新帝国，最终将从欧洲东南部一直延伸至今天的印度。

公元前335年，也就是亚历山大成为马其顿国王的第二年，亚里士多德返回雅典，自办吕克昂学园*，这一命名来源于上课的公共地点。他在此教授政治学、物理、诗学、逻辑学等科目。但亚历山大大帝于公元前323年去世，再度导致政治动荡。雅典的民意变得对马其顿人不利。亚里士多德与马其顿的关系广为人知，因此他被迫流亡，直到公元前322年与世长辞。

而亚里士多德的遗产长存。2 000多年后，他的思想依然适用。

《政治学》的主要内容

在《政治学》中，亚里士多德提出生活在有着相似目标的政治共同体中能让人变得更好。"更好"指的是更具美德：更公平、更公正、更慷慨。他还认为，拥有这些美德会让人更加幸福。因此，和他人保持密切联系是一种"自然"行为，因为这能让我们更幸福。

但什么是社会组织的最佳方式？

在《政治学》中，亚里士多德描述了三种社会组织方式：1）一人掌握权力（君主政体），2）小团体掌握权力（寡头政体）*，3）多数人掌握权力（共和政体）*。他讨论了每种政体的理论依据，并研究了现实世界的案例，结论是贵族政体*是政府的最佳形式：即一小部分"最优"公民代表整个社会做出符合最大利益的决策。

但亚里士多德认为，这一政体在现实世界中难以有效运作，因为多数人的决策是为了实现自身利益而非共同体利益。他因此得出结论，认为最佳政体是"混合政体"*。

在亚里士多德看来，"政体"指的是决定一个社会中谁来掌权的法则。他在《政治学》中指出，在混合政体中，权力在多数人和精英之间保持平衡。每个群体制约其他群体的权力，从而让决策有益于整个共同体。亚里士多德强调法律的重要性。任何共同体的最终目的都是给其公民带来幸福*，因此必须认真编撰城邦的法律，以确保达成这一目标。他认为，尽管无法指望民众按照实现共同体幸福的方式来行事，但精心制定的法律有助于敦促人们行事富有美德。

在《政治学》中，亚里士多德还强调了教育的重要性。如果城邦教育未来公民分享其价值观，那么这些价值观则得以维系。

《政治学》的研究方法开创先河。和之前思想家不同，亚里士多德将其思想建立在现实世界实用评估的基础上。书中研究了现实世界的因素如何导致政体退化。君主政体退化为僭主政体*，贵族政体退化为寡头政体，共和政体退化为平民政体*（即公众统治，远非亚里士多德所推崇）。

亚里士多德认为，政体退化的关键因素是缺乏平衡。例如一个社会中穷人数量比富人多太多，且中产阶级无足轻重，就会自然变成平民政体。或者富人势力比其他各阶层都强大得多，就会自然变成寡头政体。

社会退化会在某一群体势力过于强大时造成派系斗争*，社会将根据这一群体利益而非整个共同体的利益来组织。派系斗争导致革命，摧毁城邦。

亚里士多德得出结论，认为社会最有可能在中产阶级占主导的情况下实现幸福。社会既不过分贫穷或过分富有，因此鲜有可能陷入派系斗争。

《政治学》的学术价值

亚里士多德因《政治学》一书成为世界上第一位政治学家。他的前辈们试图构想出诸如正义或社会的理想或想象中的事物形式。而亚里士多德的著作则专注于现实城邦，研究现实中进行政治实践的人如何创造出政治共同体，以支持、服务、提升其公民。这一研究方法以所观察的信息分析为基础，被称作"经验主义"*，自此成为政治学的一大特征。

亚里士多德的思想深刻影响了历代思想家。"人天生是政治动物"这一著名论断持续影响着社会组织方式。他认为，人天然生活在有着共同目标的政治共同体中。

在中世纪的欧洲*（罗马帝国灭亡1 000年后的时期），人们视亚里士多德为政治学真理之源。当时的学者逐字逐句地分析其著作，试图理解他的全部思想。到了20世纪，他启发了一种政府以"善"为基础的政治哲学。这与主张政府不应干预公民生活的现代自由派*思想形成鲜明对比。

亚里士多德认为社会应使穷人和富人均受益。推而论之，他的政治思想抵制不均衡和排他主义。这一论断至今仍至关重要，定义了经济发展中的可行能力理论*，即经济发展不应只让发展中国家的民众富裕起来，而要让他们有能力追求美好生活。这也是当今发展经济学领域最重要的理论之一。

亚里士多德的思想还促进了现代社会定义分配正义*，即考虑商品在社会中进行最优分配的方式。受他启发的思想家们认为，商品应该分配给最能实现其价值的人，比如最好的长笛应该给最优秀的笛师，因为长笛的美德就在于能吹出美妙的音乐。

《政治学》具有开创性。尽管自亚里士多德提出这些观点以来，世界发生了许多变化，但这些观念至今仍适用。他启发了历代思想家。因此要了解政治思想史，读懂亚里士多德至关重要。

第一部分：学术渊源

1 作者生平与历史背景

要点

- 亚里士多德《政治学》的重要性在于它是第一部政治学著作。
- 亚里士多德出生于古希腊,一生中多数时间生活在雅典,先是师从影响卓著的古希腊哲学家柏拉图*,后自己办学。
- 雅典曾是一个城邦,即由一个城市及其周边领土组成的小型共同体。城邦委托给为整个共同体利益考虑的公民来统治。

为何要读这部著作?

亚里士多德《政治学》据称写于公元前335—323年,是第一部将政治学作为科学的著作。和之前思想家不同的是,亚里士多德的观点有证据作支撑。他的老师柏拉图专注于理想型和理论上的政治共同体,而亚里士多德则关注人类社会如何在真实世界中最有效地运作。

在本书中,亚里士多德描绘了人类生活在城邦的自然状态,所谓城邦就是包括城市及城市周边的共同体。他认为,"人天生是政治动物",[1] 生存的需要为共同体的形成创造了初始动力。同时他还认为,生活在城邦或政治共同体能让公民更幸福、更有美德。

所谓"美德",亚里士多德指的是养成卓越的性格,其中一个重要方面就是管理冲动的能力。例如,节制饮食是一种美德,因为这说明一个人能够管理其食欲。走近他人并交流观点能鼓励个人更有美德。在支持美德生活方式的环境里生活得有美德,能让人们幸福。

到了20世纪，美德伦理学家*复兴了政治共同体是人类幸福来源的观点。思想家们引入了培养公正、慷慨等良好品质是人类幸福基础的概念。这一观点启发了20世纪80年代用可行能力理论研究经济发展。该理论认为，经济发展应改善受其影响的人们的生活水平，帮助他们培养能让人们更幸福的品质。

> "他似乎从未怀疑，作为希腊人生活在小城邦是人类存在的最高形式，且值得长期投入大量智力资源来研究这一城邦。"
>
> ——马尔科姆·斯科菲尔德：《亚里士多德导论》

作者生平

亚里士多德于公元前384年出生于今希腊东北部斯塔吉拉。幼年时名医父亲尼各马可去世，17岁时母亲菲斯提斯去世。父母的朋友、他的监护人"将这位年轻人交给了柏拉图"，当时柏拉图已是哲学界的重要人物。亚里士多德被送往雅典，在柏拉图学园[2]学习哲学，在那里待了20年——先当学生后当老师——直到柏拉图公元前347年去世才离开。

许多在这里学习的雅典学子都将这段教育视作终生从政的训练，亚里士多德则不然。他投身于哲学本身，"将余下生命致力于哲学讨论，致力于培养智力美德的生活方式"。[3]亚里士多德的客籍民身份或许在某种程度上产生了影响。"客籍民"在雅典语中指的是外国居民。尽管受人尊敬，但外侨却无法参加政治生活，且强制缴纳特殊税。

柏拉图去世后，马其顿腓力二世国王*聘请亚里士多德担任其子亚历山大的老师，此后亚历山大征服了古代世界的大片领土，史称亚历山大大帝。和菲利普、亚历山大及马其顿的关联将影响亚里士多德的余生。

50岁时，亚里士多德返回雅典，自办学校，名为"吕克昂"。学校原本蒸蒸日上，但13年后雅典与马其顿爆发冲突，亚里士多德表示支持马其顿的统治，因此被雅典人放逐，不久与世长辞。

创作背景

亚里士多德生活在希腊古典时期*末期，彼时艺术与哲学欣欣向荣。城邦主导了希腊古典时期的政治生活。城邦统治着一个城市及其周边领土。他的出生地斯塔吉拉就是一个城邦，雅典也是。他一生中多数时间生活、工作在雅典。他从未怀疑"生活在小城邦是人类存在的最高形式"，认为这值得保护和反思。[4]

英国历史学家保罗·卡特利奇*写道："在1 000多个高度独立的希腊城邦中，亚里士多德的《政治学》以超过150个城邦的研究为基础。"这些城邦环绕地中海，延伸至小亚细亚（今土耳其）[5]，其统治方式各不相同。平民政体*和寡头政体（由一小部分人来统治）"是应用范围最广的两种政体。"[6]

亚里士多德在《政治学》中用"政体"一词表示决定谁来执政的法则，这是该著作的重要主题之一。

现代选民或许难以辨识亚里士多德时期的民主。一个民主城邦"是由有着明确的荣誉和义务的成年男性公民组成的强大共同体。"任何非成年男性公民都是社会的二等成员，不得享有投票权。[7]男性公民有参与民主公民大会的权利（和义务），有参军抵抗其他城邦的义务（和权利）。

然而在亚里士多德时期，这一城邦模式已在衰落。马其顿在腓力二世和亚历山大大帝的统治下崛起，威胁将希腊纳入同一统治者的管辖。马其顿人一步步征服了希腊各城邦，将它们纳入希腊帝国＊。曾盛极一时的公民大会沦为市政会。亚历山大于公元前323年去世，但他征服的领土从意大利延伸到印度，宣告了古典时代的终结。

亚里士多德在亚历山大去世一年后离世，正值古典时代与罗马帝国交替、希腊文明鼎盛的时期，希腊化时代就此开启。

---

1. 亚里士多德：《政治学》，70，第3卷，第6章，载《雅典政治与政体》，史蒂芬·埃弗森编，《剑桥政治思想史文本》，丛书编辑雷蒙德·戈伊斯及昆廷·斯金纳，剑桥：剑桥大学出版社，1996年，$1278^b/19$—20。
2. 卡罗·纳塔利：《亚里士多德：生平与学园》，普林斯顿：普林斯顿大学出版社，2013年，第11页。
3. 纳塔利：《亚里士多德》，第19页。
4. 马尔科姆·斯科菲尔德："亚里士多德导读"，载《剑桥希腊和罗马政治思想史》，克里斯托弗·罗威等编，剑桥：剑桥大学出版社，2000年，第317页。
5. 保罗·卡特利奇："希腊政治思想：历史背景"，载《剑桥希腊和罗马政治思想史》，克里斯托弗·罗威等编，剑桥：剑桥大学出版社，2000年，第21页。
6. 卡特利奇："希腊政治思想"，第21页。
7. 卡特利奇："希腊政治思想"，第17页。

2 学术背景

要点

- "政治"指的是"城邦的事物"。政治哲学探寻的是人类与政治共同体如何产生关联。
- 极具影响力的哲学家、亚里士多德老师柏拉图的老师苏格拉底*关注公正等美德的本质,而亚里士多德则更关注美德在现实世界中如何得以维系。
- 前苏格拉底*哲学家认为哲学是对自然世界的研究,对研究人类政治的兴趣比不上亚里士多德。

著作语境

亚里士多德在《政治学》中提出了"政体"的概念,即决定一个社会中谁掌权的法则。

英国历史学家保罗·卡特利奇*写道,古希腊人"出于实际和理论原因,用实用道德充实或实施政治。"换句话说,希腊政治概念认为,政治参与本身就是一件好事。[1] 政治哲学家瑞恩·巴洛特*指出,"古代思想家认为,城邦应该为其公民提供道德和情感教育、性格培养以及适当的宗教参与",政治生活和个人生活在很大程度上密不可分。[2]

鉴于政治结构和个人生活联系如此密切,古希腊政治哲学的最大关切就是寻求理想政体。一个城邦可实行君主政体*(由国王统治),或贵族政体(由一小部分非常合适的人统治),或共和政体(由全体公民统治)。也就是说,政体可将权力置于一人、少数人或所有人之手。

《政治学》中，亚里士多德认为理想共同体应当以贵族政体为基础，即由最优秀、最适合的人代表整个共同体的利益来统治。但他同时认为这难以实现，因为统治者倾向于考虑自身利益而非他人利益。

> "凡人认为神也有出生，穿自己的衣服，有声音，有身体。"
>
> ——色诺芬尼:《残篇》

学科概览

亚里士多德按照希腊哲学的两个传统来写作：一是前苏格拉底传统，二是柏拉图传统。

英国学者 A. A. 朗*认为，前苏格拉底哲学家"事事都要叙述一番"。为了发现事物真正的本质，他们研究自然而非神话。³ 他们的关注点更接近当今的科学而非哲学。然而在他们做研究的时代，这两种思维方式的区别并不明晰。

最著名的前苏格拉底哲学家之一色诺芬尼*批判了希腊宗教，该教教徒信奉众神，众神因住在奥林匹斯山而被称为奥林匹亚*。他认为希腊人按照自己的形象创造了众神："但如果……马……有手，那么马就会将它们的神描绘成马的形态。"⁴ 他认为，有一种单一的、深层次的"力量"或"单一的神"可由人类、风、树等所有事物共享。

和前苏格拉底哲学家不同，苏格拉底对伦理而非自然界产生了哲思。他本人未写下只言片语，而是他人为其著书，尤其是他著名的学生柏拉图。柏拉图写了数本苏格拉底对话集、散文集，书中人物（通常包括苏格拉底本人）讨论道德问题。

和前苏格拉底哲学家一样，苏格拉底也想探索事物真正的本质。他想探寻真正的正义。在柏拉图对话录的《高尔吉亚篇》中，苏格拉底说："我认为自己是少数掌握了真正政治技艺并真正从政的雅典人，因为我在每个场合的演讲都不是为了自满而是为了最好。"[5] 柏拉图展现了苏格拉底的愿望，即希望政治实现改善城邦公民生活的首要功能。

学术渊源

尽管亚里士多德受柏拉图影响最大（并通过柏拉图受到苏格拉底的影响），但他对前苏格拉底哲学家的研究同样影响了其思考。他认为，"研究自然"是一项重要事业，尽管对其研究方法持异议。

前苏格拉底哲学家关注事物的"真正的本质"，不关注事物的所为。对他们而言，下雨"不过是构成事实本质的物体的巧合行为。"[6] 他们无意了解下雨的原因及对其他事物的影响。

亚里士多德则相反，他关注事物的行为。在其著作《物理学》中，他概括出决定世界运作的"四因"，其中最重要的是"目的因"，即事物存在的原因，比如橡果的目的因就是成为橡树。[7] 也就是说，前苏格拉底哲学家主要思考物质，而亚里士多德则思考行为。

正如苏格拉底一样，亚里士多德对人性有关的问题颇感兴趣。但前者研究的是智慧和正义等美德的本质，而后者研究的是如何在人类社会维系这些品质。

1. 保罗·卡特利奇:"希腊政治思想:历史背景",载《剑桥希腊和罗马政治思想史》,克里斯托弗·罗威等编,剑桥:剑桥大学出版社,2000年,第12页。
2. 瑞恩·巴洛特:《希腊政治思想》,牛津:布莱克韦尔出版社,2006年,第4页。
3. A. A. 朗:"早期希腊哲学的范畴",载《剑桥早期希腊哲学史指南》,剑桥:剑桥出版社,1999年,第10页。
4. 大卫·萨克斯:"色诺芬尼",载《古希腊世界词典》,牛津:牛津大学出版社,1995年,第267页。
5. 柏拉图:《高尔吉亚篇》,罗宾·沃特菲尔德译,牛津:牛津世界经典系列,1995年,521d6—9。
6. 托马斯·布莱克森:《古希腊哲学》,奇切斯特:韦利—布莱克韦尔出版社,2011年,电子书。
7. 亚里士多德:《物理学》,罗宾·沃特菲尔德译,牛津:牛津世界经典系列,2008年,第5卷,第1章,1031a。

3 主导命题

要点 🗝

- 古希腊哲学家的最大关切是解答"什么是社会的最佳组织形式"这一问题。
- 柏拉图笔下的"乌托邦"*指的是不可能存在的天堂。
- 亚里士多德没有将这一无法实现的天堂理论化,而是用实证来评估社会的不同组织形式。

核心问题

和柏拉图一样,亚里士多德在书中问道:"什么是社会的最佳组织方式?"为了有效地组织社会,了解社会要实现的目标十分重要。

在其另一部名著《尼各马可伦理学》的最后部分,亚里士多德这样描述政治和个人的善之间的关系:"政治的目的就是最好的目的;政治的主要关切就是培养公民特定的品格,使他们向善且行为高尚。"[1]

政治的目的是实现人的提升,这似乎是希腊思想家的共识。人的提升通过法律来实现,或者按照亚里士多德的说法:"通过法律,我们能够变善。"[2]

《政治学》中,亚里士多德认为,如果生活在守法社会可让人变善,那么哲学家主要任务就是研究出应实施何种法律,因为哲学家认为政治是通过制定支持道德行为的法律来提升人性的艺术。这和成为政治家不同。加利福尼亚大学哲学教授多萝西娅·弗雷德认为,"亚里士多德不仅给法律赋予了最高教育权威,同时还赋予了相应的执行权。"³ 也就是说，亚里士多德认为一个城邦的政体（其政府形式和法律）是塑造公民的最强大力量。政体是美好生活的关键。

> "我们的前辈将立法留给我们来研究，因此或许最好由我们自己来研究立法，并从总体上研究政体，从而尽最大能力完成关于人性的哲学研究。"
>
> —— 亚里士多德：《尼各马可伦理学》

参与者

亚里士多德的老师柏拉图在其著作《理想国》中问道："什么是正义的本质？"《理想国》一书是苏格拉底对话集，写的是苏格拉底和其他人物的对话。柏拉图在该书中提出，"正义"只存在于有着完美政体的城邦。柏拉图臆想出一个完全公正的城邦，称之为"美丽城邦"*。

柏拉图认为，在美丽城邦中，包括妻子、儿童在内的所有财产均应共享，军队中男女性别平等。这些安排太过特殊，因此柏拉图认为这种社会只能在"哲学家成为国王来统治"，或者当政国王成为哲学家的情况下才可实现。⁴ 但他也认为，如果任何一个城邦能将这些特殊法律一一执行，将是一种乌托邦式的存在，是一种想象中的完全正义。

关于柏拉图描述美丽城邦的意图，至今仍有争议。有学者认为，柏拉图所言的美丽城邦是一个完全公正的真实城市蓝图。也有人认为其描述仅仅为了引发探讨。不论何种情况，柏拉图都认为，哲学王*是仁慈僭主政体的理想形式。

当代论战

亚里士多德受柏拉图的影响最大，他提出了柏拉图《理想国》里同样的问题，即"什么是城邦统治的最佳政体？"柏拉图的目标是"探寻何种政治共同体最有助于最有能力的人实现想要的生活。"[5]这与亚里士多德的目标相关联，即了解何种政体最能让人有道德地生活。

亚里士多德还继承了柏拉图的重要观点。苏格拉底的辩论伙伴在《理想国》里说道："难道你不知道，有的城邦实施僭主政体，有的实施平民政体，有的实施贵族政体？"[6]

亚里士多德在《政治学》里采用了相似的分类。事实上，他直接呼应了柏拉图在《理想国》中提出的一个观点。在《政治学》第2卷中，他驳斥了所有财产共有的观点。[7]但这恰恰体现了是柏拉图塑造了亚里士多德的作品。诚然，亚里士多德反对和赞同的柏拉图观点同等重要。

英国精神哲学家史蒂芬·埃弗森*认为，亚里士多德之所以反对柏拉图的完美政体，是因为柏拉图"对理论化有着毫无防备的热情"。[8]

柏拉图倾向于凭空找答案，"即使试图帮助他人获得真理，同样有可能让人远离真理。"亚里士多德的理论更有理有据。他的目标是如何将理论用于现实世界，而非只应用于纯粹哲学领域。[9]

1. 亚里士多德:《尼各马可伦理学》,第 10 卷,第 9 章,载《雅典政治与政体》,史蒂芬·埃弗森编,《剑桥政治思想史文本》,丛书编辑雷蒙德·戈伊斯及昆廷·斯金纳,剑桥:剑桥大学出版社,1996 年,3—7,1099^b/30。
2. 亚里士多德:《尼各马可伦理学》,3—7,1180^b/25—27。
3. 多萝西娅·弗雷德:"亚里士多德伦理学的政治特征",载《剑桥亚里士多德〈政治学〉指南》,剑桥:剑桥大学出版社,2013 年,第 16 页。
4. 柏拉图:《理想国》,载《剑桥政治思想史文本》,G. R. F. 法拉利编,丛书编辑雷蒙德·戈伊斯及昆廷·斯金纳,剑桥:剑桥大学出版社,2003 年,472e。
5. 亚里士多德:《政治学》,30—31,第 2 卷,第 1 章,载《雅典政治与政体》,史蒂芬·埃弗森编,《剑桥政治思想史文本》,丛书编辑雷蒙德·戈伊斯及昆廷·斯金纳,剑桥:剑桥大学出版社,1996 年,1270^b/27—28。
6. 柏拉图:《理想国》,338d。
7. 亚里士多德:《政治学》,31—32,第 2 卷,第 2 章,1271^a/10。
8. 史蒂芬·埃弗森:"引言",载《雅典政治与政体》,史蒂芬·埃弗森选编,《剑桥政治思想史文本》,丛书编辑雷蒙德·戈伊斯及昆廷·斯金纳,剑桥:剑桥大学出版社,1996 年,第 xiii 页。
9. 埃弗森:"引言",第 XIII 页。

4 作者贡献

要点

- 亚里士多德认为，人的幸福可以通过政治结社实现，即生活在有政治组织的共同体中。他认为寻找到这种政治组织的方式是通过研究各种政体。
- 在亚里士多德之前，"纯粹理想主义"（而非研究现实世界）在政治哲学中占主导地位。
- 在逻辑上，《政治学》与《伦理学》一脉相承。在《伦理学》中，亚里士多德提出了政治结社培养美德这一理论。

作者目标

在《政治学》中，亚里士多德评估并研究了不同政体，目的是为了找到最能让人生活幸福的政体。他在另一本著作《尼各马可伦理学》中写道："我们的前辈将立法留给我们来研究，因此我们最好研究政体，从而尽最大能力完成关于人性哲学的研究。"[1] 亚里士多德在《政治学》中对政体部分进行了研究。值得一提的是，《政治学》被认为是亚里士多德的讲稿。[2] 持这一观点的学者认为，该书以亚里士多德在吕克昂学园的教学讲稿为基础。而吕克昂学园则是"雅典重要的高等教育中心"，[3] 亚里士多德在此培养了雅典和其他城邦的未来领导人。

鉴于学生的类型，亚里士多德选择重点研究现实政体，或多或少摒弃了其师柏拉图的乌托邦思想模式也就不足为奇了。亚里士多德不是要培养未来的哲学家，而是未来的政治家和将军。《政治学》

或许是其讲稿合集，而非亚里士多德打算出版的作品，这一事实也对本书写作方式产生了影响。

> "那么你是否认为，如果无法表明能找到一个和演讲中提及的一模一样的城邦，我们的讨论就不尽如人意？"
> ——柏拉图：《理想国》

研究方法

《政治学》中，亚里士多德的目标是"寻找对全民来说最优的政体"。[4] 和前辈思想家一样，他也认为法治社会能让人过上好的或者更好的生活。此前包括柏拉图在内的思想家们提出了"完美城邦"的理论。但这些城邦并不存在，只是主观想象的纯粹哲学范畴。亚里士多德在书中研究了关于完美城邦的旧理论，同时研究了"其他政体……如真实存在的、管理良好的政体。"[5] 也就是说，亚里士多德的方法更科学，他从证据出发，发现对公民最有益的政体。

在这一政治哲学新方法中，亚里士多德摒弃了探寻"理想"方法的理论努力，而是研究如何创造稳定的政治共同体，以便让公民获益。他用证据来支持这一方法。柏拉图认为所有财产都应均享，而亚里士多德则回顾了历史，指出曾有统治者尝试颁布法令，规定"城邦公民应财产均等"。

亚里士多德表示，这一法令导致许多人的财产多于其习惯拥有的数量，让公民"生活要么奢侈，要么赤贫"，反过来会造成政治动荡。[6] 从依据而不是抽象理论出发，亚里士多德对财产均等的益处进行了评估。

时代贡献

要充分理解《政治学》，就必须理解《尼各马可伦理学》的最后几章。这本著作首次提出通过本性、习惯和卓越的有机结合实现人类幸福。[7]亚里士多德认为，人对美德有着深层次需求，但为了实现这一需求，人不仅要践行美德，其所处的环境也要支持并加强美德行为。他指出法律制定者"应当激励人们追求卓越，敦促他们为了高尚的动力取得进步"。也就是说，由于多数人不会自发成为高尚的人，因此国家制定法律来改善人性，并强制人们变得更好。[8]

不少学者认为，《尼各马可伦理学》最后一部分体现了亚里士多德从思考伦理学转向思考政治。《政治学》和《伦理学》之间存在逻辑联系，是因为亚里士多德认为，通过政治共同体和良好政体，人可以变得更有美德（这是道德的客体）。他在《伦理学》结尾写道："在研究了这些［政体］之后，我们才能较好地理解何种政体是最好的，每种政体的优劣排序，以及它必须采用何种法律和风俗。"[9]这是"实用的智慧"，即考虑伦理问题及其影响。将理论与实际经验相结合，这一创新塑造了政治理论的传统。

---

1. 亚里士多德：《尼各马可伦理学》，7，第10卷，第9章，载《雅典政治与政体》，史蒂芬·埃弗森编，《剑桥政治思想史文本》，丛书编辑雷蒙德·戈伊斯及昆廷·斯金纳，剑桥：剑桥大学出版社，1996年，$1181^{b}/11-15$。
2. 史蒂芬·埃弗森："引言"，载《雅典政治与政体》，史蒂芬·埃弗森编，《剑桥政治思想史文本》，丛书编辑雷蒙德·戈伊斯及昆廷·斯金纳，剑桥：剑桥大学

出版社，1996年，第 X/XI 页。
3. 约翰·帕特里克·林奇:《亚里士多德的学园：希腊教育机构研究》，伯克利：加利福尼亚大学出版社，1972年，第46页。
4. 亚里士多德:《政治学》，30，第2卷，第1章，载《雅典政治与政体》，史蒂芬·埃弗森编，《剑桥政治思想史文本》，丛书编辑雷蒙德·戈伊斯及昆廷·斯金纳，剑桥：剑桥大学出版社，1996年，1260b/25—31。
5. 亚里士多德:《政治学》，30，第2卷，第1章，1260b/25—31。
6. 亚里士多德:《政治学》，43—46，第2卷，第7章，1266b/1—40。
7. 亚里士多德:《政治学》，184—185，第7卷，第13章，$1332^a/8—1332^b/10$。
8. 亚里士多德:《尼各马可伦理学》，3—7，第10卷，第9章，1180a/7—8。
9. 亚里士多德:《尼各马可伦理学》，3—7，第10卷，第9章，1181b/20—23。

第二部分：学术思想

5 思想主脉

要点

- 亚里士多德认为生活在政治社会中是人的自然状态。
- 他认为政治结社能使人更公正,并为共同利益努力。
- 关于《政治学》的结构,学者们至今仍有争论。

核心主题

《政治学》有三个核心主题:

- 目的论(Teleology)*。"Telos"的意思是"目的",按照目的论原则,所有事物都由其最终状态决定。例如种子要变成植物,这一目的决定了它的性质。每个政治共同体也是为了实现特定目的而存在。
- 美好生活。亚里士多德论证了什么是美好生活,以及如何实现。
- 政治共同体的政体(即决定权力如何分配的规则)。亚里士多德评估了不同形式的政体,以及何种政体能最好地为公民服务。

以上三个核心主题共同构成了亚里士多德的总体论断:人的终极目的就是在政治共同体中变得更具美德。他的名言"人生来就是政治动物"正是这一含义。[1] 一个人的"自然状态"就是和其他人产生联系,人可以在政治共同体中获得幸福。因此亚里士多德认为,政治共同体会自然形成,其法律保障公民品德的提升从伦理上来讲也是正确的。

亚里士多德在《政治学》中讨论了三种不同政体:一人统

治、少数人统治、多数人统治。亚里士多德认为，每种政体既有正宗形式，也有"变态"形式。当统治者为整个城邦考虑时，就是正宗政体。当统治者仅为了一己私利时，就是变态政体。好的政体包括君主政体（一人统治）、贵族政体（少数人统治）、宪政共和政体（多数人统治）。坏的政体包括僭主政体（一人统治）、寡头政体（少数人统治）、平民政体（多数人统治）。他指出，并非一开始就这样区分，他只是扩充了柏拉图提出的观点。[2]

> "每个城邦都是某种共同体，每个共同体的建立都是为了实现某种善，因为每个人的活动都是为了实现其所认为的善。但如果所有共同体都为了实现某种善，那么最高级别的城邦或者政治共同体能包罗万象，其目标是实现最高的善，高于其他任何共同体。"
> —— 亚里士多德：《政治学》

思想探究

亚里士多德在《政治学》的开篇提出了目的论："每个城邦都是某种共同体，每个共同体的建立都是为了实现某种善。"[3] 他简要描述了政治共同体如何形成：首先是男女、奴隶主与奴隶、儿童与"家庭"的"自然"结合。几个家庭组合起来，能够更有效地满足"基本生活需求"。[4] 随着更多家庭组合到一起，形成了更大的社会，满足生活的"基本需求"绰绰有余。这时候，这些家庭将"为了更好的生活"继续联合。[5]

但什么是亚里士多德所认为的"美好生活"？

人不仅仅从群居生活中寻找满足感，同时通过与他人分享观点，培养出好坏、正义与非正义的概念。[6] 亚里士多德认为，政治、善和正义都是人性和人类智慧的产物，通过互相交流观点得以实现。他认为，"政治社会的存在应以高尚的行为为目的。""高尚的行为"指追求正义，共同实现"共同利益"。[7]

政治是确定"共同利益"的手段。亚里士多德认为，社会产品的分配应该有利于所有公民而非富人的利益。[8] 他以笛师为例，认为应该给最佳笛师按照其演奏能力配备最佳风笛。政治这一机制可用来激励人们为了共同利益而努力。

语言表述

政治学专业的学生在阅读《政治学》时需注意以下几个问题：

首先，《政治学》不是孤立的作品。亚里士多德在《尼各马可伦理学》中就美好生活和目的论进行了很多探讨，这两部作品联系密切。其次，多数学者认为亚里士多德写《政治学》并非为了出版。美国政治学家卡恩斯·洛德*表示，最常见的推测是认为亚里士多德的作品"以在吕克昂学园的讲课稿为基础"。[9]

德国古典学者、著名的亚里士多德研究学者维尔纳·耶格尔*认为，《政治学》甚至不是一套连贯的讲稿。《政治学》各卷是之后汇总的，因为第4至6卷论述了亚里士多德关于现实政府的务实论断，而其他几卷（1至3卷、7至8卷）更多停留在理论层面。[10]

洛德不同意耶格尔的观点，他认为《政治学》有可能不是讲稿，而是给学生的参考资料。按照这一解释，书中前后不一致之处是因为学生注释和誊写错误，"很难和亚里士多德本人早期添加的内容区分开来。"[11]《政治学》的行文结构和方法至今仍存在争论。

1. 亚里士多德:《政治学》,70,第 3 卷,第 6 章,载《雅典政治与政体》,史蒂芬·埃弗森编,《剑桥政治思想史文本》,丛书编辑雷蒙德·戈伊斯及昆廷·斯金纳,剑桥:剑桥大学出版社,1996 年,$1278^b/19$—20。
2. 亚里士多德:《政治学》,93,第 4 卷,第 2 章,$1289^b/45$—46。
3. 亚里士多德:《政治学》,11,第 1 卷,第 1 章,$1252^a/1$—2。
4. 亚里士多德:《政治学》,12,第 1 卷,第 1 章,$1252^b/30$。
5. 亚里士多德:《政治学》,12,第 1 卷,第 1 章,$1252^b/31$。
6. 亚里士多德:《政治学》,14,第 1 卷,第 1 章,$1253^a/10$—15。
7. 亚里士多德:《政治学》,76,第 3 卷,第 9 章,$1281^b/18$。
8. 亚里士多德:《政治学》,80,第 3 卷,第 12 章,$1282^a/39$—40。
9. 卡恩斯·洛德:"亚里士多德《政治学》特征及构成",《政治理论》第 9 卷,1981 年第 4 期,第 461 页。
10. 维尔纳·耶格尔:《亚里士多德发展史纲要》,理查德·罗宾森译,牛津:牛津大学出版社,1948 年,第 283—285 页。
11. 洛德:"亚里士多德《政治学》特征及构成",第 474 页。

6 思想支脉

要点

- 亚里士多德认为,以中产阶级为基础的政体(即由中产阶级统治的城邦)在现实中最有可能让公民更有美德。
- 派系斗争*,或财富多寡造成的共同体分裂,会导致城邦政体的衰败。
- 亚里士多德认为公共的、普及的教育有助于维护政体的稳定。

其他思想

《政治学》解释了政治生活的重要性,描述了如何组织共同体。"我们不仅要考虑什么是最优政体,也要考虑什么是可能实现的,也是所有人最容易实现的。"[1]

城邦如何改善其组织和治理?《政治学》4至6卷阐述了如何将政治理论运用到现实世界。

要理解亚里士多德的论点,必须理解政治作为科学和政治作为技术(艺术)的区别。在此,"艺术"不是指绘画等文化形式,而是指木匠活和砖瓦活等手艺。英国学者史蒂芬·埃弗森在其介绍亚里士多德著作集的书中写道:"人掌握了技术就能实现某些事情,例如医生掌握了医药技术就能带来健康。"在亚里士多德看来,"政治学家能造就城邦。"[2]

亚里士多德主要研究了如何成就一个优秀城邦的理论,其次研究了这些理论如何能产生现实中的城邦,也就是政治的技术。

> "最优的往往无法实现,因此真正的立法者和政治家不应只关注抽象范畴的最佳政体,还要思考符合实际的最佳政体。"
>
> —— 亚里士多德:《政治学》

思想探究

亚里士多德在《政治学》中发问:"对多数城邦而言,什么是最佳政体?对多数人而言,什么是最好的生活?"

他提问的背景在现实中确实存在。[3] 其中一个考虑因素是城邦的混合社会构成,"有极富阶层,有极穷阶层,还有[中间]阶层"。[4] 各阶层所占比例不同会让各城邦的情况大相径庭,从而采取不同政体。他认为,"穷人数量超过一定比例,就自然产生平民政体。"富裕阶层的权力过大时,则产生寡头政体。[5]

穷人或富人数量过多都会产生深层次问题,富人变得贪婪,穷人变得卑微。处在社会两级的民众正义观扭曲时,派系*就会出现,接踵而来的是革命和城邦的毁灭。

亚里士多德认为,为了避免人们把追逐个人欲望和优势放在首要位置而导致社会扭曲,最佳政体应该围绕中间阶层来组建,因为"其他阶层都会受到派系影响。"没有派系斗争的政治共同体更能在共同利益上实现团结。[6] 中间阶层的公正观也更加平衡。他们不会"觊觎他人的物品,他人也不会垂涎他们的物品。"中间阶层既能发号施令,也能遵守命令,且并不排斥被人发号施令。[7]

亚里士多德关于以中间阶层为基础的观点既不是寡头政

体*（由一小部分富有的精英统治），也不是平民政体*（由享有辩论和投票权的成年男性统治），而是结合了上述两种形式的共和政体。

在这部书中，亚里士多德的信念——现实世界里中间的总是最好的贯穿始终。

被忽视之处

学者们往往忽视了《政治学》中关于教育的讨论。亚里士多德在第8卷中提出了关于城邦教育的论断。[8]他认为，统治者有必要教育儿童，让他们学习技能和美德，以维持良好政体。既然"整个城邦有着同一个（目标），那么显而易见，应该给所有人提供统一教育，且教育应该是公共的而非私人的。"[9]

亚里士多德认为，在理想社会中，城邦应给所有公民的子女提供均等教育机会。他认为教育和城邦的特征有重要关联，因为"平民政体的特征创造了平民政体，寡头政体的特征创造了寡头政体，特征越优良，政体越修明。"[10]因此城邦可以通过教育投入来塑造其后代的秉性。这一体系可被视作教化手段，确保公民不抗拒城邦权力。它同时也可被视作一项平等、解放式的提议，保证城邦公民享有一定程度的教育。

近期学者强调亚里士多德关于教育的论述，认为这是其通篇论述的重要组成部分。[11]比利时学者皮埃尔·德斯特雷*指出，教育教给人城邦价值，从而帮助城邦居民实现发展："正是因为我们是'政治动物'，需要生活在城邦中，通过分享某些价值观和共同参与传达价值观的活动而满足对幸福的渴望，所以我们生活的城邦必须提供这样的生活方式。"[12]

1. 亚里士多德:《政治学》,92,第4卷,第1章,载《雅典政治与政体》,史蒂芬·埃弗森编,《剑桥政治思想史文本》,丛书编辑雷蒙德·戈伊斯及昆廷·斯金纳,剑桥:剑桥大学出版社,1996年,$1288^b/36$—38。
2. 史蒂芬·埃弗森:"引言",载《雅典政治与政体》,史蒂芬·埃弗森编,《剑桥政治思想史文本》,丛书编辑雷蒙德·戈伊斯及昆廷·斯金纳,剑桥:剑桥大学出版社,1996年。
3. 亚里士多德:《政治学》,92,第4卷,第1章,$1294^b/25$—27。
4. 亚里士多德:《政治学》,107,第4卷,第11章,$1295^b/1$—22。
5. 亚里士多德:《政治学》,109,第4卷,第12章,$1296^b/24$—27。
6. 亚里士多德:《政治学》,108,第4卷,第11章,$1296^a/7$。
7. 亚里士多德:《政治学》,108,第4卷,第11章,$1295^b/29$—30。
8. 亚里士多德:《政治学》,195—207,第8卷。
9. 亚里士多德:《政治学》,195,第8卷,第1章,$1337^a/21$—23。
10. 亚里士多德:《政治学》,195,第8卷,第1章,$1337^a/16$—18。
11. 皮埃尔·德斯特雷:"教育、休闲与政治",载《剑桥亚里士多德〈政治学〉指南》,玛格丽特·德斯劳列尔与皮埃尔·德斯特雷编,剑桥和纽约:剑桥大学出版社,2013年,第301—323页。
12. 德斯特雷:"教育",第306页。

7 历史成就

要点

- 尽管《政治学》启发了许多政治思想家，但人们依然批评亚里士多德没有提出如何实现其所有观点的详细方案。
- 亚里士多德是雅典的杰出教师和知识分子。
- 亚里士多德关于"自然奴隶"的论述让一些现代读者不悦，但也有人认为他实际上是在谴责奴隶制。

观点评价

《政治学》中，亚里士多德将其最理想的政治结构愿景置于现实世界的藩篱中。他旨在探寻如何提高共同体民众的生活水平，在某种程度上，他确实实现了这一目标。亚里士多德提出了一些核心要点，如社会的目标是什么、社会类型有哪些、何种社会最有助于提高公民生活水平。

然而，有些思想家认为《政治学》是一部未竟之作。亚里士多德关于城邦安排的阐释缺乏一个重要因素，即教育体系。

加利福尼亚大学哲学教授多萝西娅·弗雷德认为，亚里士多德"针对公民的教育计划仅遗憾地停留在儿童音乐教育规划蓝图。"[1] 弗雷德对此提出了两个可能的解释。可能是更完整的版本有部分遗失了，也有可能是亚里士多德决定不开展这一浩大工程。要把构成成功教育系统的所有要素都列举出来，这几乎是不可能完成的任务。

> "亚里士多德的自然奴隶理论至少是一个潜在的批判理论。认真思考这一理论的奴隶主应扪心自问：'我的奴隶真的是自然奴隶吗？还是他太精明、目的性太强？'"
> —— 马尔科姆·斯科菲尔德："亚里士多德奴隶论的意识形态及哲学"

当时的成就

如果真如大家广泛认为的那样，《政治学》是由亚里士多德在吕克昂学园讲课稿重新整理而来，那就说明亚里士多德的教学对其终生都产生了影响。如果学术影响力不够，那么他的讲课稿也难以留存。

逍遥学派保存了亚里士多德的著作，这一学派或许是根据亚里士多德边踱步边教学的风格而得名。亚里士多德去世后，学生们继续推进他的事业，吕克昂学园和逍遥学派传统仍有重要影响。据美国历史学家大卫·C. 林德伯格*描述，亚里士多德去世后，其密友提奥夫拉斯图斯*"成为吕克昂学园的掌门人。"[2]

尽管提奥夫拉斯图斯继续了亚里士多德的研究，但他唯一流传的作品却主要关于植物学和地质学。亚里士多德著作及吕克昂学园图书馆的藏书遗赠给了地中海沿岸的著名学者们，最后传到了希腊哲学家、罗德岛的安德罗尼柯*之手，他"进行整理、编辑，让这些作品声名卓著、广为流传。"[3] 到了12世纪，来自如今荷兰的佛兰芒哲学家、莫尔贝克的僧人威廉*将《政治学》译成拉丁文。这让亚里士多德的思想有了更多受众，人们迅速认识到这些思想的价值。

尽管亚里士多德哲学的不少内容引起了罗马天主教会的猜忌，

但强调收集、保护和运用前人智慧的经院哲学*思想传统帮助调和了亚里士多德思想与天主教教义的关系。

局限性

《政治学》令现代读者尤为不悦的关键之处在于亚里士多德对奴隶制的捍卫，以及认为有些人是"天生的奴隶"。他认为，"动动脑子就能预料到，奴隶主和奴隶是天生的"，那些能执行其主人预见的人是"天生的奴隶"。[4]

亚里士多德认为这一安排是互利的，因为奴隶主和奴隶有着相同的目标。然而，"天生的主人"无法自己完成所有计划，"天生的奴隶"无法独立规划，需要被人指导行事。但亚里士多德反驳"契约"奴隶。他认为，不应该让一个理性的人仅仅因为不幸被俘就成了奴隶。[5]这不是互利的关系。

英国古典学家马尔科姆·斯科菲尔德*等学者认为，亚里士多德可能是以一种微妙的方式反对奴隶制。他指出，亚里士多德抨击（以抓人而实现的）"契约"奴隶，认为绝大多数人都不应受到奴隶制的束缚。毕竟，有多少人无法思考呢？他认为，亚里士多德写奴隶制是为了强迫"奴隶主扪心自问：'我的奴隶生来便是奴隶吗？还是他太过精明、目的性太强？'"[6]因此，认真诠释亚里士多德关于奴隶制的观点十分重要，也许其中暗含了对当时普遍存在的"不道德"奴隶制的批评。

1. 多萝西娅·弗雷德:"亚里士多德《伦理学》的政治特征",载《剑桥亚里士多德〈政治学〉指南》,剑桥:剑桥大学出版社,2013年,第33页。
2. 大卫·C.林德伯格:《西方科学的开端:从史前到公元1450年哲学、宗教、体制背景下的欧洲科学传统》,芝加哥:芝加哥大学,2008年,第73页。
3. 林德伯格:《西方科学的开端》,第74页。
4. 亚里士多德:《政治学》,12,第1卷,第1章,载《雅典政治与政体》,史蒂芬·埃弗森编,《剑桥政治思想史文本》,丛书编辑雷蒙德·戈伊斯及昆廷·斯金纳,剑桥:剑桥大学出版社,1996年,$1252^a/31$—34。
5. 亚里士多德:《政治学》,19,第1卷,第7章,$1255^b/12$—14。
6. 马尔科姆·斯科菲尔德:"亚里士多德奴隶论的意识形态及哲学",载《亚里士多德〈政治学〉评论文集》,理查德·克劳特与斯蒂文·斯科特蒂编,兰哈姆:罗曼与利托菲尔德出版社,2005年,第100页。

8 著作地位

要点

- 有的思想家认为,《政治学》写于两个不同时期,和中间几卷相比,早期的内容更有"柏拉图式"的色彩(更明显地受到其师柏拉图的影响)。
- 亚里士多德所有主题中都用了同样的分析方法。他将文科或理科的基本原理条分缕析,找到核心要义。
- 亚里士多德的笔触涉及诗学、物理、自然科学等多个学科。其作品在各领域都极有影响力。

定位

《政治学》的不同部分可能在不同时期完成,因此难以定位该书与亚里士多德其他作品的关系。

亚里士多德的早期作品仍受到其师柏拉图思想的影响。和之后的作品相比,这些作品包含了更多的柏拉图式概念。英国学者托马斯·凯斯*解释了柏拉图的准则,即万物都反映了完美的、超自然的"形态"。桌子仅仅是"桌子",是因为它们与"理想形态中"完美的、理论上的桌子相似。

亚里士多德则相反,他认为所有事物都是独立的。桌子并不是反映了完美、超自然的桌子。它们之所以被认为是桌子,是因为其个体特质让它们更像桌子而不是椅子。[1] 以德国古典学者维尔纳·耶格尔*为代表的思想家们得出结论,认为亚里士多德初期是柏拉图学派,随着他本人成为更有建树的思想家,他变得越来越

"亚里士多德学派"。²

《政治学》其中几卷阐述了柏拉图的政治理想（第1—3卷、第7—8卷），其他几卷则是亚里士多德对于各个政体的研究（第4—6卷）。关于《政治学》写于亚里士多德的职业生涯早期还是晚期，或是横跨这两个时期，学术界仍存在争论。

> "《政治学》被视为政治哲学最伟大的著作之一。"
> ——史蒂芬·埃弗森："引言"，《政治学》

整合

亚里士多德的研究生涯不仅仅只围绕政治，他还是位涉猎广泛的学者，对逻辑、科学、修辞*甚至诗歌均有研究。而他研究这些主题的方法一直是有分析有条理的，将任何研究主题分解成基本板块，之后运用对该学科基础版块的了解来研究其如何产生，如何最好地发展。

亚里士多德《诗学》开篇如下："我们不仅从总体上讨论诗歌，还要讨论每种类型的容纳力，优秀诗歌所需要的情节构成，以及诗歌组成部分的数量和性质……首先，让我们先从原则谈起。"³他试图理解诗歌的独特、卓越之处，以及诗歌如何变得卓越。

他对动物也按照类似的分析方式进行研究。"有的动物很简单：其智慧、肉体分割后都大差不差。"有的则分成特定的部分，让"手不再分成手，脸不再分成脸。"⁴亚里士多德将复杂的动物生活分成各个部分：手由手掌、手指和细胞组成。这一富有条理方法是亚里士多德所特有的。

意义

英国学者史蒂芬·埃弗森写道:"《政治学》是政治哲学领域最伟大的作品之一。"⁵ 而亚里士多德的其他作品也对不同学科产生了巨大影响,例如他对物理学的思考主导了17世纪前的西方科学。意大利历史学家斯特法诺·佩尔费蒂*描述了亚里士多德关于动物学*的科学研究著作在中世纪如何备受赞誉。"在13世纪中期,亚里士多德所有自然类著作"都已列入了今意大利北部帕多瓦大学学生书目。⁶

尽管后来的学者否认了亚里士多德提出的某些概念,但这并不适用于《政治学》。当今读者批判该书中某些内容,如自然奴隶以及女性的社会作用的段落。但亚里士多德《政治学》的核心思想政治归属能改善民众生活,在蒸蒸日上的当代政治理论领域仍享有核心地位。

在现代世界,亚里士多德是众多著名学者的智慧之源,如印度经济学家、诺贝尔奖得主阿玛蒂亚·森*、美国哲学家玛莎·努斯鲍姆*,甚至以正义和共同体理论闻名的美国政治哲学家迈克尔·桑德尔*也受其影响。

1.托马斯·凯斯:"亚里士多德",《亚里士多德的哲学发展:问题与前景》,威廉·罗伯特·威安斯编,伦敦:罗曼与利托菲尔德出版社,1990年,第1—2页。

2. 丹尼尔·格雷厄姆:《亚里士多德的两个体系》,牛津:牛津大学出版社,1990年,第5页。
3. 亚里士多德:《诗学》,1,第1卷,理查德·扬科译,印第安纳波利斯:哈克特出版社,1987年,47^a/1—2。
4. 亚里士多德:《动物史》,阿德莱德:阿德莱德大学出版社,电子书,https://ebooks.adelaide.edu.au/a/aristotle/history/book1.html。
5. 史蒂芬·埃弗森:"引言",载《雅典政治与政体》,史蒂芬·埃弗森编,《剑桥政治思想史文本》,丛书编辑雷蒙德·戈伊斯及昆廷·斯金纳,剑桥:剑桥大学出版社,1996年,第1页。
6. 斯特法诺·佩尔费蒂:《亚里士多德〈动物学〉及其文艺复兴时期的评论家》,鲁汶:鲁汶大学出版社,2000年,第1页。

第三部分：学术影响

9 最初反响

要点

- 针对《政治学》的批评最早集中在其过度精细、过度正式的研究方法上。
- 《政治学》在整个欧洲中世纪（约5—15世纪）被视为政治事实的权威来源，无数学者为其撰文。
- 早期近代约始于15世纪末期，那时的学者不太愿意将亚里士多德视作权威。尽管关注点相似，但他们想自己收集证据。

批评

《政治学》的出版或许并不是为了广泛传播，因此人们直到很久以后才认真作出回应。

西方思想家在13世纪重新发掘了《政治学》，对"政治思潮产生了深远影响。"[1] 尽管亚里士多德的思想启发了诸多中世纪基督教学者，但该书也招致了一些批评。

例如，意大利人文主义*学者彼特拉克*认为亚里士多德研究政治的方法太过精细和系统。亚里士多德认为，人只要理解高尚的含义就能变得高尚，并不需要对美德执着。彼特拉克不同意这一点，他认为政治生活是一个富有情感的过程，而亚里士多德则太过冷静。

他写道："亚里士多德解释了什么是美德*，但读他的著作并不能……让人心潮澎湃，并热爱美德，憎恨恶行。"[2] 但彼特拉克依然承认亚里士多德思想的重要性。他认为自己有义务找到一个立场，让亚里士多德关于"美好生活"的世俗、理性思想与基督教思想相协调，后者认为生活应当按照人神关系的本质来评判。

亚里士多德从人在世界中的实现感来描绘"美好生活"，但彼特拉克认为，如果生活中缺乏对人格化上帝的爱（与情感、喜悦有关），就不能被称为"美好"。

意大利知识分子圣托马斯·阿奎纳*等思想家认为智慧存在于多处，从而解决了这一问题。阿奎纳认为关键是通过学习汲取智慧。

> "让他们保留傲慢的见解，保留让许多无知之人欣喜的亚里士多德之名。更重要的是，让他们拥有徒劳的快乐和毫无根据的喜悦，这些都几近毁灭；简而言之，让他们拥有无知之人的利益，拥有因轻信犯错而获得的膨胀之心。"
>
> —— 彼特拉克：《关于他的无知》

回应

《政治学》最早的全面批评出现在亚里士多德去世约一千年之后，因此他本人无法作出回应。而很多思想家欣赏而非批判他的观点。当其作品在中世纪重新被发掘后，学者们将《政治学》重新包装，以适应当时的政治结构。这心照不宣地表明了对亚里士多德著作的赞赏，尽管他"未曾接受基督教的启示之光，也不了解中世纪教会的概念。"[3]

在中世纪，一场名为"经院哲学"*的运动主导了西方思潮。这一运动的目的是理解并受益于所有智慧之源，包括重新发现的经典文本和《圣经》等。运动兴起的原因很大程度上是因为中世纪学者希望亚里士多德思想与天主教教义相协调。包括阿奎纳在内的主要经院哲学思想家就《政治学》撰写评论，逐字逐句地展示亚里士多德的洞见。[4]

阿奎纳最著名的作品《神学大全》探讨了罗马天主教教义，主要目标是将政治学等世俗问题与神学*问题相结合。尽管亚里士多德并非基督徒，阿奎纳在本书中仍引用了他的观点，将他尊称为"哲学家"，推崇他的许多观点。在引用《伦理学》时，阿奎纳写道："这位哲学家认为，幸福根据完美的美德进行运作。"[5]此外，阿奎纳认为，"法律的适当效应是培养人的美德，"*从而改善守法民众的品格。[6]

冲突与共识

到了早期近代，人们对亚里士多德的态度发生了变化。尽管思想家们依然认为其观点具有启发性，但已开始借用他的方法，形成自己关于现实世界的结论。英国学者厄尼斯特·巴克*论述了在早期近代，亚里士多德对尼可罗·马基雅维利*的影响。马基雅维利是佛罗伦萨外交官和政治理论家，被称作近代政治理论的创始人。巴克认为他"从小就受到亚里士多德思想的熏陶。"[7]巴克认为，马基雅维利运用了亚里士多德的政体分类，即一人统治、少数人统治、多数人统治。

亚里士多德和马基雅维利都关心僭主如何维系权力。僭主政体是君主政体的"变态"形式，亚里士多德认为，"尽管维系权力是万事的根本，但僭主应当按照国王的角色行事，或表面上像国王一样行事。"也就是说，僭主表面上应当像一个关心臣民共同利益的统治者。[8]这与马基雅维利的著名建议不谋而合，即"成功塑造个人（慷慨）形象的统治者可享有美名。"[9]

46

然而巴克也认为，马基雅维利"并不亏欠亚里士多德"。和中世纪评论家不同，"他不将亚里士多德的普遍原理"视作权威，而是"从当下搜集事实"，得出自己的结论。[10] 此外，他还驳斥了道德和政治的关联。亚里士多德认为政治的最终目的是改善公民生活，而马基雅维利认为政治只是获取权力的方式。亚里士多德反对柏拉图的理想主义，推崇更高程度的经验主义。马基雅维利也以同样的方式反对亚里士多德的观点。

---

1. 克里斯托弗·克莱恩亨斯编，"亚里士多德与亚里士多德主义"，《中世纪意大利：百科全书》，牛津：劳特利奇出版社，2004年，第56页。
2. 彼特拉克，引自克里斯托弗·克莱恩亨斯，《中世纪意大利：百科全书》第1卷A—K，牛津：劳特利奇出版社，2004年，第117页。
3. 康纳·马丁："关于亚里士多德《政治学》的一些中世纪评论"，《历史》第36卷，1951年，第34页。
4. 圣托马斯·阿奎纳：《亚里士多德〈政治学〉评论》，理查德·J.里根译，印第安纳波利斯：哈克特出版社，2007年。
5. 圣托马斯·阿奎纳：《神学大全》，移动参考材料，2010年，1867。
6. 阿奎纳，《神学大全》，3108。
7. 厄尼斯特·巴克爵士：《柏拉图及亚里士多德政治思想》，纽约：多弗出版社，1959年，第515页。
8. 亚里士多德：《政治学》，148，第5卷，第11章，载《雅典政治与政体》，史蒂芬·埃弗森编，《剑桥政治思想史文本》，丛书编辑雷蒙德·戈伊斯及昆廷·斯金纳，剑桥：剑桥大学出版社，1996年，1314^a/39—40。
9. 尼可罗·马基雅维利：《君主论》，昆廷·斯金纳与拉塞尔·普莱斯编，剑桥：剑桥大学出版社，1988年，第63页。
10. 巴克：《柏拉图及亚里士多德政治思想》，第517页。

10 后续争议

要点

- 政治自然主义*是亚里士多德的主要观点之一,即人自然生活在城邦中。到了18世纪,爱尔兰保守派政治家埃德蒙·伯克*等思想家复兴了这一观点。
- 《政治学》启发了美德伦理学*这一当代思潮。
- 美国哲学家玛莎·努斯鲍姆将美德伦理学应用于政治。她建议政治共同体应以培养公民美德为目标。

应用与问题

《政治学》一书对中世纪政治哲学影响巨大。苏格兰哲学家 J. H. 伯恩斯*写道:"亚里士多德《政治学》和《尼各马可伦理学》的翻译"对13世纪政治思想的发展"极为重要"。[1]

早期近代*的政治思想发生了变化。亚里士多德认为,政治能让城邦公民摆脱"纯粹生活",帮助他们实现"美好生活"。然而到了约16—18世纪的早期近代*,自由主义政治哲学开始产生影响。自由主义植根于个人自由和平等,认为国家的作用在于让个人获得自由,而不是提升公民。英国政治哲学家托马斯·霍布斯*因此对《政治学》有一段著名的批评,"鲜有其他事物能比亚里士多德在《政治学》中的多数观点更让政府厌恶。"[2] 他认为,国家仅为了公民的"纯粹生活"而存在。

但自由主义*也受到批评,批评者与亚里士多德某些观点一致。1791年,爱尔兰政治家埃德蒙·伯克在其名作《反思法国大革命》中批评了法国大革命*的基石自由思潮,"亚里士多德发现……平民政体与僭主政体有许多惊人的相似之处。"³ 关于政治结社,伯克与亚里士多德观点一致,认为如果权力分配得当,所有参与者最终都能获得提升。"正如本性更善之人总应处在领导地位,当一人比其他人地位更高时,他极有可能实现完美。"⁴

> "如果我记得没错,亚里士多德认为平民政体与僭主政体有许多惊人的相似之处。我可以确定,在平民政体中,大多数公民有能力针对少数公民实施最残酷的压迫。"
> —— 埃德蒙·伯克:《反思法国大革命》

思想流派

如今,亚里士多德的伦理和道德思想是美德伦理学的关键来源之一,美德伦理学这一哲学运动关注于个人行为的道德准则。其他研究伦理学的方法包括关注个人遵循规则的道义论*,以及关注个人行为结果的结果论*。

美德伦理学强调美德。如果讨论是否该救溺水之人,"美德伦理学家会强调,帮助该人是仁慈的、乐善好施的。"⁵ 他们还会认为,仁慈、乐善好施的人是善的、富有美德的。

英国哲学家 G.E.M. 安斯科姆*是该学科最重要思想家之一。她于1958年首次出版《现代道德哲学》,使现代美德伦理学成为独立研究领域。⁶ 她和其他美德伦理学家主要关注亚里士多德的《伦理学》而非《政治学》。他们将富有美德地行事(自我培养)作为"富有道德地"行事(遵守立法者的指示)的替代版本。安斯科姆认为,伦理行为之所以富有伦理,不是因为遵循了一套既定的规则,而是因为符合一系列美德。

当代研究

美德伦理学可用于现实政治。美国哲学家玛莎·努斯鲍姆认为,伦理理论太过抽象,无法应用于现实世界。她写道:"伦理学理论脱离实际人类经验,各方对此都有不满。"

努斯鲍姆是最早将美德伦理学应用于现代政治理论的哲学家之一,她还认为亚里士多德"不仅捍卫以美德为基础的伦理理论,也推崇人类之善的单一客观描述。"[7]有的思想家认为,人和人的善并不相同。努斯鲍姆则称,亚里士多德认为存在能让所有人获益的"美好生活"生存状态,人们可通过培养美德来实现。亚里士多德还描述了需要培养的美德,为人类在现实世界中生存提供了伦理指南。他的观点可用于教育、立法等人类发展的关键领域。

努斯鲍姆本人提出了"客观人类道德的草图,这一草图基于富有美德的行为,即每个人类领域的正常运转"。换句话说,她以对人类有利这一客观事实为目标概括出一套伦理,如培养勇气、善良、慷慨等美德。

---

1. J.H. 伯恩斯:"政治学、体制及观点导读",《剑桥中世纪政治思想史》,剑桥:剑桥大学出版社,1988年,第356页。
2. 托马斯·霍布斯:《利维坦》,J.C.A. 加斯金编,牛津:牛津大学出版社,1998年,第143、445页。
3. 埃德蒙·伯克:《反思法国大革命》,纽黑文:耶鲁大学出版社,2003年,第

106 页。
4. 伯克,《反思》,第 79 页。
5. 罗莎琳德·赫斯特豪斯:《美德伦理学》,牛津:牛津大学出版社,1999 年,第 1 页。
6. G.E.M. 安斯科姆,"现代道德哲学",《哲学》第 33 卷,1958 年第 124 期,第 1—19 页。
7. 玛莎·努斯鲍姆:"非相对美德:亚里士多德研究方法",《中西部哲学研究》第 13 卷,1988 年,第 33 页。
8. 努斯鲍姆:"非相对美德",第 39 页。

11 当代印迹

要点 🔑

- 如今，人们将亚里士多德尊为让政治科学成为独立学科的创始人。
- 政治共同体应改善其民众生活成为可行能力理论的要义，该理论认为，"发展"不仅是增加一国收入。
- 有的思想家认为，可行能力理论培养的"能力"太过"西方化"，不可能客观地列出美德。

地位

德裔美国政治哲学家列奥·施特劳斯*强调《政治学》在现代的重要性，他写道："亚里士多德是政治学真正的创始人。"[1] 亚里士多德是最早从现实案例而非纯思想角度研究政治的思想家之一。

美国政治学家吉尔·弗兰克*在《差别民主制：亚里士多德及政治学著作》中写道，鉴于现代国家的规模和复杂性，人们往往认为古代哲学家"与我们的时代不相干"。弗兰克认为这是错误的做法。[2] 她还表示，因其"政治排斥"而否定亚里士多德是不明智的。所谓"政治排斥"指的是亚里士多德提倡男女不平等，"奴隶主"和"奴隶"不平等。她写道，认真阅读亚里士多德的原文十分重要，因为"更仔细的阅读能让（现代读者）更有机会了解他想表达的内容。"她指出，自20世纪后半叶以来，亚里士多德作为政治学洞见之源，人们对他的兴趣与日俱增："政治观点不同且往往对立的学者们都认为，亚里士多德的作品是当代政治的丰富来源。"[3]

施特劳斯等人认为，亚里士多德为以"最优的人"执政为基础的政治提供了正当理由。弗兰克的同僚、美国哲学家玛莎·努斯鲍姆认为，亚里士多德对教育的关注"为运转良好的自由或社会民主政权提供了基础。"⁴甚至观点不同的人士也认为亚里士多德的政治洞察超越了时代。

> "如果我们有理由渴望更多财富，那么必须问：这些理由究竟是什么，如何运作，依靠什么，以及有了更多财富之后我们能'做'什么？……收入和财富本身并（不）让人艳羡，只是因为它们是一种通用手段，让人有自由选择自己珍惜的生活方式。"
>
> ——阿玛蒂亚·森：《以自由看待发展》

互动

亚里士多德的作品启发了玛莎·努斯鲍姆的美德伦理学观点，美德伦理学也相应地激发了关于经济发展的"可行能力理论"。

诺贝尔奖*得主、印度经济学家阿玛蒂亚·森倡导可行能力理论，该方法认为，发展的最终目的应该是"让人们获得更多真正自由的过程。"⁵森认为，发展不应仅仅让国家更富裕。富裕的国家也会限制公民自由，不允许他们参加政治、获得医疗或营养。可行能力理论认为，经济发展的目标应该是提高民众的生活水平。

这一理论质疑了当时现存的发展理论。英国经济学家约翰·威廉姆森*在其1990年的论文《华盛顿的政策改革意味着什么》中列举了美国向发展中国家提供援助制定政策条件时所用的10个政策工具。⁶这些工具包括：

- 市场自由化

- 增加医疗和教育支出
- 减少赤字

这些政策聚焦于"增长、低通胀、收支平衡、收入公平分配等标准经济目标",后成为"华盛顿共识"*。这一经济研究方法优先考虑经济效益,除维持基本生活外,并未说明经济发展的目的。[7] 这与可行能力理论形成鲜明对比,后者认为经济发展是实现一国公民发展的手段。

如今,联合国开发计划署*用可行能力理论来研究经济学。它强调的不是发展中国家的国民生产总值*,而是人类发展指数*。这需要衡量成人识字率、平均寿命、人均国民生产总值等指标。[8] 也就是说,亚里士多德启发了当今经济发展的核心概念。

持续争议

可行能力理论受到了批判。有的思想家认为,不论文化背景就假定所有人都渴望普遍自由,这一推断存在问题。

英国学者大卫·克拉克*尽管支持可行能力理论*,但对其实施方法存在异议。他提出,可行能力理论应培养哪些能力?他认为森的观点太过宽泛,没有详细列出这一方法应该培养的能力目标。

美国哲学家玛莎·努斯鲍姆则相反。她以亚里士多德的美德论为基础列出清单,从另一个角度看来也存在问题——其方法过于专横。克拉克写道:"列出这一清单的唯一合理方法或许是向穷人咨询,"否则我们会认为发展应当是普遍的。而事实上,发展基于什么是美好生活这一西方观点。[9]

克拉克举了一个例子。一项调查表明,南非民众心目中的美好生活包括"工作、住房、教育、收入、家庭和朋友、宗教、健康、好衣服、娱乐和放松,[以及]安全和经济保障。"¹⁰ 努斯鲍姆则提出另一套标准:"健康、身体完整、正直、感知、想象力、思考、情感、实践理性*、从属、其他物种、玩耍、控制政治和物质环境。"¹¹

南非受访者的答案更多地关乎工作和人际关系,而努斯鲍姆则更关注个人本身的发展。

---

1. 列奥·施特劳斯:《城邦与人》,芝加哥:芝加哥大学出版社,1964 年,第 21 页。
2. 吉尔·弗兰克:《差别民主制:亚里士多德及政治学著作》,芝加哥:芝加哥大学出版社,2005 年,第 4 页。
3. 弗兰克:《差别民主制》,第 4 页。
4. 弗兰克:《差别民主制》,第 5—6 页。
5. 阿玛蒂亚·森:《以自由看待发展》,纽约:阿尔弗雷德·A. 克诺夫出版社,1999 年,第 3 页。
6. 约翰·威廉姆森:《拉丁美洲的调整:发生了什么?》,登录日期 2014 年 3 月 1 日,http://faculty.washington.edu/acs22/SinklerSite/PS%20322/What%20Washington%20Means%20by%20Policy%20Reform.pdf。
7. 威廉姆森:《拉丁美洲的调整》,2014 年 3 月 1 日。
8. 联合国:"人类发展报告",登录日期 2014 年 2 月 25 日,http://hdr.undp.org/en/statistics/hdi。
9. 大卫·克拉克:《发展愿景:人类价值研究》,切尔滕纳姆:爱德华·埃尔加出版社,2002 年,第 27 页。
10. 大卫·克拉克:"可行能力理论",载《埃尔加发展研究指南》,大卫·克拉克编,切尔滕纳姆:爱德华·埃尔加出版有限公司,2006 年,第 38 页。
11. 玛莎·努斯鲍姆:《女性与人类发展:可行能力理论》,剑桥:剑桥大学出版社,2000 年,第 78—80 页。

12 未来展望

要点 🔑

- 亚里士多德以人的提升为核心来阐述政治学,这一浩大工程至今仍是一种重要的研究方法。
- 美国政治哲学家迈克尔·桑德尔将亚里士多德的方法应用于同性婚姻,认为人们应该根据受鼓励的美德进行立法。
- 亚里士多德《政治学》一书自中世纪以来就启发着思想家,至今仍是如此。

潜力

亚里士多德在《政治学》中的观点不仅启发了关于经济发展的可行能力理论,同时也启发了其他学者将其政治思想应用于现代世界。

例如,美国学者小弗雷德·D. 米勒*认为,现代政治家应当"在现实政治中牢记亚里士多德的忠告。"[1] 也就是说,为了避免纯粹民粹主义*的民主和寡头政治,政治家们应牢记亚里士多德的"混合"政体论。

他呼应了亚里士多德观点,指出即使现代国家将政治权利分配给所有公民,经济权力往往仍集中在少数人手中。尽管现代国家享有"代议制民主下的……政治秩序……但经济秩序很大程度上还是由[一小部分掌握经济权力的人]来决定。"[2]

美国哲学家玛莎·努斯鲍姆*等思想家突出强调《政治学》中仍适用于当今世界的内容。有关政治结社的最终目标是通过政治结构实现幸福,就是其中之一。

亚里士多德的著作一直是各界政治思想家的灵感之源。强调平衡、稳定和人类发展的思想家们尤其能在他的思想中寻找共鸣。

> "美德吸引着越来越多当代哲学辩论的关注。各方对脱离具体人类实践的伦理理论都存在不满。"
> ——玛莎·努斯鲍姆:"非相关美德:亚里士多德研究方法"

未来方向

美国政治哲学家迈克尔·桑德尔按照现代世界修正了亚里士多德的观点。谈到亚里士多德对政治公正的愿景时,他写道:"公正关乎于尊崇、承认、提升和培养社会实践中蕴含的美德与善。"[3]

和亚里士多德一样,桑德尔认为,要定义某个事物,必须了解该事物的最终目的。要定义"权利",必须明确了解这些权利的目的。桑德尔哲学中体现了亚里士多德另一个重要思想,即"正义是令人尊敬的。"要制定法律、实现公正,人们要清楚"社会实践中应尊崇和奖励哪些美德。"[4] 桑德尔重新引用了亚里士多德在笛师中分配风笛的例子。最佳笛师应得到最佳风笛,因为"风笛的目的就是吹出美妙音乐。"[5]

桑德尔用另一个例子解释了关于同性婚姻的争论。有的思想家认为,在这一案例中,非歧视原则应普遍适用于婚姻。但如果在逻辑上剑走偏锋,这一原则难道不是在支持包括直系亲属、人和物品在内的任何两个实体的婚姻?为解决这问题,桑德尔认为应该提出:"哪种关于婚姻的诠释是对值得尊敬的美德的赞美?"

他引用了南非裔法官玛格丽特·马歇尔*支持同性婚姻的裁决。玛格丽特认为,否认同性婚姻是给原本有害的同性婚姻刻板印象"加盖了准许的公章",但事实上,同性关系和异性关系都应受到官方的尊重。[6]

也就是说,桑德尔体现了亚里士多德的论证有助于解决现代社会看似难解的争论。关键在于明确我们要分配什么权利或特权,以及分配的原因。

小结

亚里士多德的《政治学》具有高度原创性。作为经验分析的早期著作,该书有着开拓性意义。书中囊括了大量的反思、对比、原则及概念,至今仍对政治理论产生影响。这其中包括"美好生活"的构成,以及关于国家应在多大程度上为公民提供服务。

尽管《政治学》在古代曾被忽视,但中世纪思想家们对其重新评价,巩固了它在政治思想史上的地位,且近几十年来声望愈增。亚里士多德的思想启发了美国政治哲学家迈尔克·桑德尔、印度经济学家阿玛蒂亚·森、美国哲学家玛莎·努斯鲍姆等现代学者。这些思想家提出了关于社会运作的问题,以便让公民过上最好的生活。他们的著作确保了《政治学》的与时俱进。

对于学习政治思想史的学生而言,《政治学》仍是一本关于政治理论和古希腊政治生态的极其重要的著作。但最重要的是,该书让亚里士多德获得了世界上第一个政治学家这一美誉。

---

1. 小弗雷德·D.米勒:"亚里士多德治国之术与现代政治",《亚里士多德〈政治

学〉在今日》,雷恩·E.古德曼与罗伯特·B.塔利斯编,奥尔巴尼:纽约州立大学出版社,2008年,第30页。
2. 米勒:"亚里士多德治国之术与现代政治",第30页。
3. 迈克尔·桑德尔:"公正:该如何做是好?",《波士顿大学法律评论》第91卷,2011年,第1303页。
4. 桑德尔:"公正:该如何做是好?",第1303页。
5. 桑德尔:"公正:该如何做是好?",第1304页。
6. 桑德尔:"公正:该如何做是好?",第1307—1309页。

术语表

1. **柏拉图学园**（公元前387—86年）：由柏拉图创立、雅典学者及雅典青年才俊组成的精英俱乐部。

2. **贵族政体**：字面意思是"由最优秀的人来统治"。亚里士多德认为，由一小部分与该职位相称的人来统治，不会太过关注财富等事宜。

3. **美丽城邦**：柏拉图《理想国》中"完美"城邦之名。译为英文含义大致是"美丽城邦"。

4. **可行能力理论**：一种经济发展理论，认为成功的经济发展应根据个人能力做其所想的程度而定。

5. **古典时期**（公元前510—323年）：希腊历史上艺术、文化和哲学百花齐放的时期，古希腊因此而闻名。

6. **结果论**：伦理学的理论研究方法，认为行为的对错应根据其结果而定。

7. **政体**：在亚里士多德看来，政体是决定一个社会由谁来掌权的法则。

8. **平民政体**：字面意思为"多数人的统治"；亚里士多德认为平民政体是不可取的，因为大众会为了个人利益来统治——例如以牺牲社会凝聚力为代价，对富人过度征税。

9. **道义论**：伦理学的理论研究方法，认为行为是否道德应以其是否遵守规则或出于责任感而定。

10. **分配正义**：物品在社会中的"公正"分配。

11. **早期近代**：通常指中世纪末到工业革命之初的时期，约15世纪晚期到18世纪中期。

12. **经验主义**：认为所有知识都基于所感知的证据而非纯粹理性的理论。

13. **伦理**：规范人与人之间行为的道德原则。

14. **幸福**（Eudaemonia）：希腊词汇，"eu"意为好，"daimon"意为精神；通常指"幸福"，更恰当的理解是"人类的繁荣。"

15. **派系**：更大共同体中的小群体。

16. **派系斗争**：共同体或社会分裂成"各个派系"（为了私利的团体），通常有分歧、摩擦的含义。

17. **法国大革命**（1789—1799年）：法国政治大动荡的10年，革命者们尝试了君主立宪制、革命专政、直接民主、自由共和国等多种政权形式，最终以拿破仑·波拿巴建立军事独裁而告终。

18. **国民生产总值**：由一国公民（甚至包括生活在该国境外的公民）所生产的商品、服务的总价值。

19. **希腊化时代**：通常指亚历山大大帝公元前323年去世至罗马帝国兴起前，古希腊文明影响力的巅峰时期。

20. **希腊帝国**（公元前359—323年）：指马其顿腓力二世自公元前359年起纳入其直接管辖的一批希腊城邦。公元前333年，其子亚历山大将帝国东拓至当今印度。公元前323年，亚历山大去世，其继承人们瓜分了帝国。

21. **人类发展指数**：用一个数据体现寿命、教育、财富等一国"人类发展"总体状态的综合指数。

22. **人文主义**：强调研究古典文学的文艺复兴运动。

23. **自由主义**：以个人自由和平等思想为基础的政治哲学。

24. **吕克昂学园**：亚里士多德在雅典创办的学校，人们通常在此聚集，该地名为吕克昂。

25. **中世纪**：从罗马帝国灭亡到意大利文艺复兴的欧洲历史时期（约5—15世纪）。

26. **君主政体**：一种统治形式，通常由世袭的国王或女王享有最高权力。

27. **诺贝尔奖**：对多领域学术成就及促进世界和平进行嘉奖的国际奖项，通常被视作世界最高荣誉之一。

28. **寡头政体**：字面意思是"少数人的统治"。亚里士多德认为，寡头政体是由一小部分富人统治的不良政体，因为他们往往从自身利益出发，忽视穷人利益，牺牲社会凝聚力。

29. **奥林匹亚**：古希腊的众神。众神有着拟人化色彩（长相或行为与人类相似），且经常显示自然的一面（如雷神宙斯），或社会的一面（如婚姻之神赫拉）。

30. **哲学王**：柏拉图心目中理想城邦的理想统治者。只有哲学家真正理解正义，因此必须将其理解应用于治理。

31. **城邦**：古希腊时期的城邦。城邦通常由公民本体来统治，即根据特定政体来组织。

32. **政治自然主义**：认为人会自然进行政治结社，而非普遍认为的人类远离自然的理论。

33. **共和政体**：由公民统治；亚里士多德认为这是最佳政体。

34. **民粹主义者**：指试图迎合多数人的人，常作贬义用。

35. **实践理性**：理性与行动的关联（而非纯粹进行理论思考，与行动脱节）。关注实践理性的哲学家们会思考真实世界中什么是正确的，不会对抽象概念进行纯理论思考。

36. **前苏格拉底哲学**：生活在古希腊或临近时期、未受到苏格拉底影响的哲学学派，专注于解释自然世界的实质。

37. **修辞**：劝说的艺术和理论，书面语和口语皆可。

38. **经院哲学**：源于中世纪大学和宗教机构的思潮。这一学派探究智慧之源（如哲学家、神学家、圣经等），以揭示知识。

39. **目的论**：对历史事件、行为或物体的理解，认为其因为特定目的存在，而非为了其因存在，也非某种力量造就了其存在。

40. **神学**：关于宗教原则的系统、学术研究。

41. **僭主政体**：由一人统治，出于个人利益而牺牲社会稳定。

42. **联合国开发计划署**：成立于1965年的联合国系统内执行部门，致力于减贫及增强全球卫生、提高识字率、促进民主等更广义的人类发展目标。

43. **乌托邦**：天堂或完美之地，通常无法实现。

44. **美德伦理学**：伦理学的一种研究方法，关注人的行为，而不是人遵守的规则（"义务论"）或行为的后果（"结果论"）。

45. **美德**：亚里士多德用"美德"来指性格的卓越和有效管理冲动。（例如节制饮食是一种美德，因为这要求对自己的身体进行有效约束。）

46. **华盛顿共识**：约翰·威廉姆森提出的概念，包含10个常见的改革政策建议，由华盛顿特区的金融机构针对发展中国家制定，并由美国政府推动。宏观经济稳定、经济自由化和减贫是这些政策强调的重点。

47. **动物学**：针对动物的科学研究。

人名表

1. 马其顿王国亚历山大三世（通常称作"大帝"）（公元前356—323），马其顿国王，在其父征战欧洲的基础上，将帝国拓展至非洲和亚洲，直到在巴比伦逝世。

2. 罗德岛的安德罗尼柯（约公元前60年），继亚里士多德后担任吕克昂学园院长，出版了新版亚里士多德著作，以及《物理学》《伦理学》《范畴学》评论。

3. 格特鲁德·伊丽莎白·玛格丽特·安斯科姆（1919—2001），出生于爱尔兰的英国哲学家。她在美德伦理学领域的著作，尤其是《现代道德哲学》，被视作该学科的奠基之作。

4. 圣托马斯·阿奎纳（1225—1274），意大利知识分子和圣人，倡导"自然神学"，试图通过自然推理来证明上帝的存在。

5. 瑞恩·巴洛特，加拿大多伦多大学政治哲学家，主要关注古代哲学如何启迪现代民主。

6. 厄尼斯特·巴克（1874—1960），英国学者，主要研究古代政治思想。他在现代背景下重新诠释了古典哲学思想，从而成为20世纪该领域最重要的英国思想家之一。

7. 埃德蒙·伯克（1729—1797），爱尔兰政治家及政治思想家，在英国担任议员多年。其作品涉猎广泛，其中包括对法国大革命的著名批判。

8. J. H. 伯恩斯，苏格兰思想史哲学家，在伦敦大学学院工作多年，关注中世纪政治哲学、民主中的程序问题等多领域研究。

9. 保罗·卡特利奇（1947年生），英国历史学家，专注希腊研究，尤其是古斯巴达历史及文化。

10. 托马斯·凯斯（1844—1925），英国学者，牛津大学莫德林学院道德哲学研究员。

11. 大卫·克拉克，剑桥大学发展学讲师，专注研究人类发展及文化问题。

12. 皮埃尔·德斯特雷，比利时鲁汶大学古代历史与哲学教授，专注研究柏拉图和亚里士多德。

13. 史蒂芬·埃弗森，英国约克大学精神哲学讲师。

14. 吉尔·弗兰克，美国南卡罗来纳大学学者，专注研究古典政治理论。

15. 多萝西娅·弗雷德（1941年生），加利福尼亚大学伯克利分校哲学教授，亚里士多德《伦理学》著名评论家。

16. 托马斯·霍布斯（1588—1679），英国政治哲学家，其著名论断包括：政治秩序是人造的，生命本质上是"可悲、肮脏、残忍、短暂的"。

17. 维尔纳·耶格尔（1888—1961），德国古典学者，因将柏拉图与亚里士多德思想联系起来而著名。他认为亚里士多德将柏拉图思想应用于实际。

18. 大卫·C.林德伯格（1935—2015），美国科学哲学家，专注研究中世纪及文艺复兴时期科学史，1999年获得科学史学会颁发的最高奖项萨顿奖章。

19. 安东尼·阿瑟·朗（1937年生），加利福尼亚大学伯克利分校的英国古典学者。

20. 卡恩斯·洛德（1944年生），美国海军战争学院战略领导力教授，研究历史上获得政治权威的不同方式。

21. 尼可罗·马基亚维利（1469—1527），意大利佛罗伦萨外交官、政治思想家、政治家，其著作《君主论》被视作现代政治理论的首部著作。

22. 玛格丽特·马歇尔（1944年生），南非裔律师和法官，马萨诸塞州

最高法院首位女法官。

23. 小弗雷德·D.米勒，鲍林格林州立大学哲学荣誉教授，研究亚里士多德。

24. 玛莎·努斯鲍姆（1947年生），美国哲学家，专注研究美德伦理学，20世纪复兴亚里士多德热潮的重要人物，对美德伦理学和发展学中的女性主义尤为关注。

25. 斯特法诺·佩尔费蒂，比萨大学中世纪及古代史教授，专注研究亚里士多德的影响。

26. 彼特拉克（弗郎西斯科·彼特拉克）(1304—1374)，意大利学者和诗人，为西塞罗古典著作在欧洲文艺复兴时期的发现和普及做出了贡献。

27. 马其顿腓力二世（公元前382—336），今希腊北部马其顿王国国王，带领马其顿征服希腊，在统一希腊大部分地区并开始入侵波斯时遇刺。

28. 柏拉图（公元前428—348），古希腊哲学家，或许是西方历史上最伟大的哲学家。其哲学涵盖正义、爱、形而上学等多个主题，为几个世纪的追随者们确定了研究方法。

29. 迈克尔·桑德尔（1953年生），美国政治哲学家，以正义及共同体理论家身份最为著名。

30. 马尔科姆·斯科菲尔德，剑桥大学古典学教授，专注研究古代政治思想。

31. 阿玛蒂亚·森（1933年生），印度经济学家，1998年因在福利经济学领域的贡献获诺贝尔奖，在剑桥大学、牛津大学、哈佛大学任教。

32. 苏格拉底（公元前470—399），古希腊哲学家，从未出版过个人著作，但其身边的人（尤其是柏拉图）广泛传播了他的思想。其著作奠定了西方哲学的基础。

33. 列奥·施特劳斯（1899—1973），德裔美国政治哲学家，专注研究古典哲学史，试图从"伟大作品"中挖掘永恒智慧，在保守思想家中尤为出众。

34. 提奥夫拉斯图斯（公元前371—287），继亚里士多德之后成为吕克昂学园校长，因植物分类最为著名。

35. 莫尔贝克的僧人威廉（1215/35—1286），佛莱芒中世纪翻译家、哲学家，因将希腊语医学及科学文本译为拉丁语而著名，当时拉丁语为受过教育的人所使用，希腊语所用的人更少。

36. 约翰·威廉姆森（1937年生），英国经济学家兼国际政治家，因提出"华盛顿共识"而闻名，即国际金融机构在20世纪80年代所提倡的支持自由市场的组合政策。他还曾为联合国、世界银行、国际货币基金组织担任顾问。

37. 色诺芬尼（公元前570—475），苏格拉底前希腊哲学家和讽刺作家，因批判崇敬上帝和运动征服等希腊信仰而著名。

WAYS IN TO THE TEXT

KEY POINTS

- Aristotle (384–322 B.C.E.) was an ancient Greek philosopher.
- In his text *Politics*, believed to have been written between 335 B.C.E. and 323 B.C.E., he argues that political communities create the necessary conditions in which mankind can flourish.
- Aristotle's ideas remain persuasive today.

Who Was Aristotle?

Aristotle, the author of *Politics*, was a philosopher. He was born in 384 B.C.E. in Stagira, a city in the Kingdom of Macedonia in the northeastern part of the Greek peninsula. At the age of 17, he went to Athens, the center of learning in the classical Greek world, to study with the philosopher Plato*—whom many people considered to be the greatest thinker in the Western tradition. Aristotle remained a student at Plato's Academy* until 348 B.C.E.

In 343 B.C.E., he returned to Macedonia to become the personal tutor of the young Alexander the Great,* a man who would later conquer vast territories in Mediterranean Europe, including Greece, North Africa, and Asia.

The political structure of Greece underwent dramatic changes during these years. For centuries, the *polis**—the small city-state and its surrounding territories—had dominated Greek political life. But the Macedonian rulers had begun to build an empire that would eventually stretch from southeast Europe all the way to what today is India.

In 335 B.C.E., the year after Alexander became the king of Macedonia, Aristotle returned to Athens. He established his own school, The Lyceum,* named after the public meeting place where lessons were held. There, he lectured his students on subjects that included politics, physics, poetics, and logic. But the death of Alexander the Great in 323 B.C.E. brought renewed political instability. Popular opinion in Athens turned against the Macedonians. Aristotle's connection with Macedonia was well known, and he was forced into exile, dying in 322 B.C.E.

Yet Aristotle's legacy certainly endures. Well over 2 000 years later, his ideas continue to remain relevant.

What Does *Politics* Say?

In *Politics*, Aristotle says that living in a politically organized community of citizens sharing similar goals can make people better human beings. By "better", he means more virtuous: more fair, more just, and more generous. Aristotle also argues that possessing these virtues makes people happier. So, he says, living in close association with other people is a "natural" behavior, because it has the capacity to make us happier.

But what is the best way to organize a society?

In *Politics*, Aristotle describes three ways in which societies are organized: 1) power in the hands of one person (kingship), 2) power in the hands of a small group (an oligarchy),* and 3) rule in the hands of the many (a polity).* He discusses the theoretical arguments for each of these forms of rule and looks at real-world examples, concluding that the best form of government would be rule by an aristocracy: * a small group of the "best" citizens, who would make decisions in the best interests of society as a whole.

Aristotle says, however, that this form is unlikely to work successfully in the real world because most people make decisions that further their own interests rather than the community interest. As a result, he concludes, the best form of government would be a "mixed constitution*."

For Aristotle, "constitution" refers to the laws determining who holds power within a society. In a mixed constitution, he notes in *Politics*, power is balanced between the many and the elite. Each group limits the other's power, allowing decisions to be made that benefit the whole community. Aristotle emphasizes the importance of the law. The ultimate purpose of any community is to bring happiness ("eudaemonia"*) to its citizens, so the laws that governed the *polis* would have to be written carefully to ensure they furthered that goal. Aristotle says that although people cannot be relied on to behave in a way that furthers community happiness, carefully considered laws can help prompt them to behave in a virtuous way.

He also highlights the importance of education in *Politics*. If the state educated its future citizens, teaching them to share in its values, those values would be maintained.

Politics was groundbreaking in its approach. Unlike previous thinkers, Aristotle based all his ideas on a practical assessment of how they would play out in the real world. In the book, he examines how real-world factors can lead a constitution into decline. A kingship can degenerate into a tyranny.* An aristocracy can degenerate into an oligarchy. A polity can degenerate into a democracy* (that is, rule by the public—far from Aristotle's favored system).

Aristotle argues that the key factor that makes a constitution degenerate is imbalance. For example, a society with too many poor people relative to the number of rich people, with a negligible middle class, will naturally become a democracy. Or, when the rich are too powerful in relation to the other classes, a society will naturally become an oligarchy.

The problem with degenerate societies is that they create factionalism,* which occurs when a single group becomes too powerful. Society then becomes organized in a way that serves the interests of that group, rather than the interests of the community as a whole. And factionalism leads to revolutions, which destroy the state.

Aristotle concludes that societies are most likely to achieve happiness if middle classes dominate them. Being neither very poor nor very rich, these societies are unlikely to degenerate into factionalism.

Why Does *Politics* Matter?

It is thanks to *Politics* that Aristotle has become known as the world's first political scientist. His predecessors had tried to imagine ideal or imaginary forms of things like justice or society. In contrast, Aristotle's work focuses on actual city-states. He asks how real people practicing politics in the real world can create political communities that support, serve, and improve their citizens. This approach, based on the analysis of observable information, is known as "empiricism"* and has been a feature of political science ever since.

Aristotle's thinking has had a profound influence on thinkers throughout history. His famous statement that "man is a political animal" has ongoing implications for the way societies are organized. He meant that it is natural for people to live within political communities and to share common goals.

In the European Middle Ages* (the period of about a thousand years following the fall of the Roman Empire), people regarded Aristotle as a source of truth about politics. The scholars of the day analyzed his works line by line, as they sought to understand all his ideas. In the twentieth century, he inspired a political philosophy based on the *good* that a government can achieve. This was in contrast to modern liberal* thought, according to which, government should not interfere in the lives of its citizens.

Aristotle argued that society existed to benefit both the rich and the poor. As a result, his political thought led to a rejection of the politics of imbalance and exclusion. This argument remains vitally important today. It has helped define the Capability Approach* to economic development, according to which, economic development should not just make developing countries richer but should also enable the people in those countries to pursue a good life. This is one of the most important theories in the field of development economics today.

Aristotle's ideas have also helped to define modern attitudes to distributive justice*—a consideration of the ways in which goods should best be shared out within a society. Thinkers inspired by Aristotle argue that the goods should go to those who can best realize their worth. In other words, the best flutes should go to the best flute players, for example, because the virtue of flutes is to produce beautiful music.

Politics was groundbreaking. Despite the changes in the world that have occurred since Aristotle conceived his ideas, its concepts are still relevant now. Aristotle inspired political thinkers throughout history. As a result, to understand the history of political thought, it is vital to understand Aristotle.

SECTION 1
INFLUENCES

MODULE 1
THE AUTHOR AND THE HISTORICAL CONTEXT

KEY POINTS

* Aristotle's *Politics* is relevant because it was the first work of political science.
* Aristotle was born in ancient Greece. He spent most of his life in Athens, first as a student of the enormously influential Greek philosopher Plato* and then running his own school.
* Athens was a *polis*—a small community composed of a city and its surrounding territories. The government of the *polis* was entrusted to citizens who worked for the good of the whole community.

Why Read This Text?

Aristotle's *Politics* is believed to have been written between 335 B.C.E. and 323 B.C.E. It is famous for being the first work to deal with politics as a science. Unlike earlier thinkers, Aristotle based his ideas on evidence. The philosopher Plato, Aristotle's teacher, focused on an ideal, theoretical, political community. In contrast, Aristotle was interested in how human societies could best function in the real world.

In the text, Aristotle describes how the natural condition of humanity is to live in the *polis*, the community dwelling in the city and the city's environs. "Man is by nature a political animal," he thinks.¹ For him, the needs of survival create the initial impetus for forming a community. But Aristotle also believes that living in a *polis* or political community can make its citizens happier and more virtuous.

By "virtue,"* Aristotle means possessing excellence of character. One key aspect of this is a person's ability to manage his impulses. To eat moderately, for example, is virtuous because it shows an individual can manage his appetite. Living close to, and exchanging views with, other people encourages individuals to become more virtuous. And living virtuously—within an environment that supports virtuous living—makes people happy.

In the twentieth century, virtue ethicists* revived this belief that the political community is the source of human happiness. These thinkers introduced the concept that human happiness is based on developing good qualities—justice, generosity, and so forth. This belief, in turn, inspired the Capability Approach* to economic development of the 1980s, which held that economic development should improve the life chances of those it affects and help them to develop the qualities that will make them happier.

> *"He never seems to have doubted that being Greek and living in a small* polis *was the supreme form of human existence, nor that the study of the polis was worth the investment of huge intellectual resources over a long period."*
>
> —— Malcolm Schofield, *"Aristotle: An Introduction"*

Author's Life

Aristotle was born in Stagira, in what is now northeastern Greece, in 384 B.C.E. His father Nicomachus, a notable physician, died when Aristotle was a child. By the time Aristotle was 17, his mother, Phaestis, had also died. Aristotle's guardian, a friend of his parents, "handed over the young man to Plato"—who was already a significant figure in the world of philosophy. Aristotle was sent to Athens to study philosophy at Plato's Academy[*2] where he stayed for the next 20 years—first as a student and then as a teacher—only leaving after Plato's death in 347 B.C.E.

Many of the Athenian students at the academy viewed their education as training for a life spent in the practice of politics. Aristotle did not. He threw himself into philosophical education for its own sake, devoting "the rest of his life to philosophical discussions and to a way of life dedicated to the cultivation of the intellectual virtues."[3] Aristotle's status as a metic* may have partly influenced that. "Metic" was the Athenian term for a resident foreigner. Although often well-respected members of the community, metics were excluded from participating in political life and forced to pay special taxes.

After Plato's death, King Philip II* of Macedon hired Aristotle to tutor his son Alexander, who would later become known, after conquering huge swathes of the ancient world, as Alexander the Great.* This connection with Philip, Alexander, and Macedonia would affect the rest of Aristotle's life.

At 50, Aristotle returned to Athens and founded his own school, The Lyceum.* It flourished, but after 13 years, conflict broke out between the Athenians and the Macedonians. Aristotle had expressed support for Macedonian rule. As a result, the Athenians forced him into exile. He died soon after.

Author's Background

Aristotle lived at the end of the Classical period* of Greek history, a time defined by the flowering of art and philosophy. The *polis** dominated the political life in Classical Greece. *Polites* (pronounced "polities"), the plural of *polis*, were city-states that ruled over a city and its surrounding territories. Stagira, Aristotle's birthplace, was a *polis*. So was Athens, where Aristotle lived and worked for most of his life. He never doubted that "living in a small *polis* was the supreme form of human existence," worth protection and reflection.[4]

"Aristotle's *Politics*," writes the British historian Paul Cartledge,* was "based on research into more than 150 of over 1,000 separate and jealously independent Greek polites." These city-states ringed the Mediterranean and stretched into Asia Minor (modern Turkey).[5] But they were not all ruled in the same way. Democracy* and oligarchy* (rule by a small group of people) "were the two most widespread forms of constitution."*[6]

Aristotle uses "constitution" in *Politics* to refer to the laws deciding in whose hands power should be led: one of the work's key themes.

Democracy in Aristotle's time would not be recognizable to the modern voter. A democratic *polis* "was a strong community of adult male citizens with defined honors and obligations."Anyone who was not an adult male citizen was a second-class member of society and was denied the privilege of the vote.[7] Male citizens had the right (and obligation) to participate in democratic citizen assemblies and also had the obligation (and privilege) to join military campaigns against other city-states.

In Aristotle's time, however, this model of the city-state was in decline. The rise of Macedon under Philip II and Alexander the Great threatened to bring Greece together under a single ruler. One by one the Macedonians conquered the Greek city-states and incorporated them into their Hellenistic Empire.* The once-powerful citizen assemblies became little more than town councils. Alexander died in 323 B.C.E. But his conquests—stretching across the known world, from Italy to India—spelled the end of the Classical era.

Aristotle died a year after Alexander, just as the Hellenistic Age*—the period between the Classical age and the Roman period, when Greek cultural influence was at its peak—was beginning.

---

1. Aristotle, *Politics*, 70. Book III, Chapter 6, in *The Politics and The Constitution of Athens*, ed. Stephen Everson of *Cambridge Texts in the History of Political Thought*, series editors Raymond Geuss and Quentin Skinner (Cambridge: Cambridge University Press, 1996), $1278^{b}/19-20$.
2. Carlo Natali, *Aristotle: His Life and School* (Princeton: Princeton University Press, 2013), 11.
3. Natali, *Aristotle*, 19.
4. Malcolm Schofield, "Aristotle: An Introduction," in *The Cambridge History of Greek and Roman Political Thought*, ed. Christopher Rowe et al (Cambridge: Cambridge University Press, 2000), 317.
5. Paul Cartledge, "Greek Political Thought: The Historical Context," in *The Cambridge History of Greek and Roman Political Thought*, ed. Christopher Rowe et al (Cambridge: Cambridge University Press, 2000), 21.
6. Cartledge, "Greek Political Thought," 21.
7. Cartledge, "Greek Political Thought," 17.

MODULE 2
ACADEMIC CONTEXT

KEY POINTS

- "Politics" means "things of the city." Political philosophy explores the ways in which people relate to political communities.
- Socrates*—the enormously influential philosopher who taught Aristotle's teacher, Plato—was interested in the true nature of virtues, such as justice. Aristotle was more interested in how virtues could be supported in the real world.
- Pre-Socratic* philosophers, or the philosophers who preceded Socrates, saw philosophy as an inquiry into the natural world. They were less interested in studying human politics than Aristotle was.

The Work in its Context

Aristotle's book *Politics* is concerned with the concept of "constitutions": * the laws determining who holds power within a society.

Writing about the Ancient Greeks, the British historian Paul Cartledge* argues that "for both practical and theoretical reasons they enriched or supplemented politics with practical ethics." In other words, the Greek conception of politics was that *political participation is in itself a good thing*.[1] "Ancient thinkers," writes the political philosopher Ryan Balot,* "believed that the *polis* should provide for the ethical and emotional education, character development, and appropriate religious participation of its citizens" and that political life and personal life were bound up in one another to an enormous degree.[2]

Given that political structures and personal lives were so entwined, the over-riding concern of political philosophy in ancient Greece was to find the ideal constitution. A city could be ruled as a monarchy* (by a king), as an aristocracy* (by a small group of particularly appropriate people), or the polity* (the citizens as a whole). In other words, the constitution could place power in the hands of one person, a few people, or everyone.

In *Politics*, Aristotle argues that the ideal community would be based on an aristocracy, by which he means the best, most suitable people, tasked with governing in the interests of the whole community. He says, however, that this is unlikely to happen; rulers tend to rule for their own sake, rather than for the sake of others.

> "Mortals suppose that gods are born, wear their own clothes and have a voice and body."
>
> ——Xenophanes, *Fragments*

Overview of the Field

Aristotle was writing in two traditions of Greek philosophy: the Pre-Socratic* tradition and the Platonic* tradition.

The British scholar A. A. Long* says that the pre-Socratic philosophers were interested in "giving an account of all things." To discover the true nature of things, they studied nature, rather than myths.[3] Their interests were closer to what is now called science, rather than what is now called philosophy. At the time they were working, however, the distinction between these two ways of thinking was not clearly defined.

One of the most famous pre-Socratic philosophers, Xenophanes,* criticized Greek religion, the followers of which believed in a group of gods called the Olympians* because they lived on Mount Olympus. He argued that the Greeks invented the gods in their own image: "But if... horses... had hands then horses would portray their gods as horses."[4] Xenophanes believed there was a single, underlying "force" or "one god" that was shared by all things—from human beings, to wind, to trees.

Unlike the pre-Socratics, Socrates did not philosophize about the natural world, but about ethics. He did not write anything himself; others, notably his student, Plato,* wrote about him. Plato wrote several Socratic dialogues, prose works in which characters (usually including Socrates himself) discuss moral problems.

Like the pre-Socratics, Socrates wanted to discover the true nature of things. His concern was to find true justice. In Plato's dialogue *Gorgias*, Socrates says: "I believe that I'm one of a few Athenians... to take up the true political craft and practice the true politics. This is because the speeches I make on each occasion do not aim at gratification but at what's best."[5] Plato shows that Socrates wanted politics to fulfill its primary function: to improve the lives of those in the *polis*.

Academic Influences

Although Aristotle's most important influence was Plato (and, through Plato, Socrates), his study of the pre-Socratics also influenced his thinking. He believed these "inquirers into nature" were doing a very important job, yet he disagreed with their methods.

The pre-Socratics focused on the "true nature" of things, rather than looking at what things did. To a pre-Socratic, rain falling from the sky "is really nothing more than the coincidental behavior of the objects that constitute the nature of reality."[6] They were not interested in why rain fell from the sky or in the effect that it had on other things when it did so.

In contrast, Aristotle was concerned with the way things behaved. In his work *Physics*, he outlines "four causes" that he believes determine the way in which the world functions. The most important is Aristotle's "final cause": the reason why a given object exists. The acorn's *final cause*, for example, is to become an oak tree.[7] In other words, while the pre-Socratics were primarily concerned with speculating on the material of the world, Aristotle was concerned with action in the world.

Like Socrates, he was interested in questions that relate to humanity. But while Socrates examined the nature of virtues such as wisdom and justice, Aristotle examined how these qualities could be supported within human societies.

---

1. Paul Cartledge, "Greek Political Thought: The Historical Context," in *The Cambridge History of Greek and Roman Political Thought*, ed. Christopher Rowe et al (Cambridge: Cambridge University Press, 2000), 12.
2. Ryan Balot, *Greek Political Thought* (Oxford: Blackwell, 2006), 4.
3. A.A. Long, "The Scope of Early Greek Philosophy," in *The Cambridge Companion to Early Greek Philosophy* (Cambridge: Cambridge University Press, 1999), 10.

4. David Sacks, "Xenophanes," In *A Dictionary of the Ancient Greek World*. Oxford (Oxford University Press, 1995), 267.
5. Plato, *Gorgias*, trans. Robin Waterfield (Oxford: Oxford World's Classics, 1995), 521d6–9.
6. Thomas Blackson, *Ancient Greek Philosophy* (Chichester: Wiley-Blackwell, 2011), ebook.
7. Aristotle, *Physics*, trans. Robin Waterfield (Oxford; Oxford World's Classics, 2008), Book V, Chapter 1, 1031a.

MODULE 3
THE PROBLEM

KEY POINTS

* A key concern for the philosophers of Ancient Greece was to answer the question, "Which is the best way of organizing society?"
* Plato wrote about a "utopia"*—that is, an impossible paradise.
* Instead of theorizing about an unachievable paradise, Aristotle used evidence to assess different ways of organizing society.

Core Question

In his book *Politics*, Aristotle, like Plato, asks the question, "What is the best method of organizing society?" To organize society effectively, it is important to know what that society wants to achieve.

In the final section of another of his famous works, the *Nicomachean Ethics*, Aristotle had written about the relationship between politics and individual goodness: "The end of politics is the best of ends; and the main concern of politics is to engender a certain character in the citizens and to make them good and disposed to perform noble actions."[1]

This idea that politics exists to improve man appears to be common among Greek thinkers. The method by which humanity is to be improved is through laws, or in Aristotle's words, "It is through laws that we can become good."[2]

In *Politics*, Aristotle argues that if men become good by living in law-abiding societies, then the primary task of the philosopher is to work out which laws should be in place—believing that politics is the art of improving humanity through making laws that support ethical behavior. This is not the same as being a statesman. Dorothea Frede,* a professor of philosophy at the University of California, says that "Aristotle attributes to the laws not only the supreme authority in education, but also the respective executive power."[3] In other words, Aristotle believes that a state's constitution (its form of government and its laws) is the most powerful force shaping its citizens. The constitution is the key to the good life.

> *"Now our predecessors have left the subject of legislation to us unexamined; it is perhaps best, therefore, that we should ourselves study it, and in general study the question of the constitution, in order to complete to the best of our ability the philosophy of human nature."*
>
> ——Aristotle, *Nicomachean Ethics*

The Participants

Aristotle's teacher Plato, in his most famous work, *The Republic*, had posed the question "What is the nature of justice?" Plato wrote *The Republic* as a Socratic dialogue between Socrates and various other characters. In it, Plato argues that "justice" is only found in a city with a perfect constitution. Plato imagines a perfectly just city, which he calls "Callipolis"* (roughly, "Beautiful City").

In Callipolis, Plato theorizes, all property (including wives and children) would be held in common, and the sexes would have equality in the military. These arrangements were so unusual that Plato believed such a society could only come about if "philosophers rule as kings" or if existing kings become philosophers.[4] But Plato argues that if any city did enforce all of his unusual laws it would be a kind of utopia—an imaginary place of perfect justice.

There is still debate about Plato's intentions in describing Callipolis. Some scholars believe that he meant Callipolis to be a blueprint for a real city of perfect justice. Others argue that his description was simply intended to provoke interest in the argument. In either case, Plato is making a case for a philosopher king* as an idealized form of benevolent tyranny.

The Contemporary Debate

Influenced by Plato above all others, Aristotle's *Politics* raises some of the same questions as Plato's *Republic*. Both books ask, "What is the perfect constitution for the rule of a city?" Plato's aim was "to consider what form of political community is best of all for those who are most able to realize their idea of life."[5] This goal is related to Aristotle's main goal: to understand which constitution best supports people in living ethically.

Aristotle also takes on some of Plato's key ideas. "Don't you know," says one of Socrates' debating partners in *The Republic*, "some cities are ruled tyrannically,* some democratically,* and some aristocratically?"*[6]

Aristotle uses similar categories in *Politics*. In fact, he responds directly to one idea that Plato puts forward in *The Republic*. In Book II of his *Politics*, he dismisses the idea that all property should be shared in common.⁷ But this helps to show that Plato shaped Aristotle's project. Indeed, the aspects of Platonic thought that Aristotle chose to reject are as important as the ideas he shared.

The British philosopher of the mind Stephen Everson* argues that Aristotle rejects Plato's version of the perfect constitution because of Plato's "unguarded enthusiasm for theorizing."⁸ Plato's tendency to dream up answers to his questions out of thin air is "as likely to take one away from the truth as it is to help one to attain it." Aristotle keeps his theory much more grounded. His objective is to consider how his theory would work in the real world, rather than in the realm of pure philosophy.⁹

---

1. Aristotle, "Nicomachean Ethics: Book X, Chapter 9," in *The Politics and The Constitution of Athens*, ed. Stephen Everson of *Cambridge Texts in the History of Political Thought*, series editors Raymond Geuss and Quentin Skinner (Cambridge: Cambridge University Press, 1996), 3–7 1099^b/30.
2. Aristotle, "Nicomachean Ethics," 3–7, 1180^b/25–27.
3. Dorothea Frede, "The Political Character of Aristotle's Ethics," in *The Cambridge Companion to Aristotle's Politics* (Cambridge: Cambridge University Press, 2013), 16.
4. Plato, *The Republic*, in *Cambridge Texts in the History of Political Thought*, ed. G.R.F. Ferrarri, series editors Raymond Geuss and Quentin Skinner (Cambridge: Cambridge University Press, 2003), 472e.
5. Aristotle, *Politics*, 30–31. Book II, Chapter 1, in *The Politics and The Constitution of Athens*, ed. Stephen Everson of *Cambridge Texts in the History of Political Thought*, series editors Raymond Geuss and Quentin Skinner (Cambridge: Cambridge University Press, 1996), 1270^b/27–28.
6. Plato, *The Republic*, 338d.
7. Aristotle, *Politics*, 31–32. Book II, Chapter 2. 1271^a/10.
8. Stephen Everson, "Introduction," in *The Politics and The Constitution of Athens*, ed. Stephen Everson, *Cambridge Texts in the History of Political Thought*, series editors Raymond Geuss and Quentin Skinner (Cambridge: Cambridge University Press, 1996), xiii.
9. Everson, "Introduction," XIII.

MODULE 4
THE AUTHOR'S CONTRIBUTION

KEY POINTS

- Aristotle believed humanity could achieve happiness through political association—that is, through living in communities with a political organization. He thought the way to find this kind of political association lay in studying constitutions.*
- Before Aristotle, "pure idealism" dominated political philosophy—not the study of the real world.
- *Politics* logically follows Aristotle's work *Ethics*, in which he developed his theory that political association enables the development of virtue.

Author's Aims

In *Politics*, Aristotle evaluates and studies different constitutions, aiming to identify which one best enables people to live well. In another work, *Nicomachean Ethics*, Aristotle wrote that "our predecessors have left the subject of legislation to us unexamined; it is perhaps best therefore to study the question of the constitution, in order to complete to the best of our ability the philosophy of human nature."[1] Aristotle carried out this investigation into the constitution in *Politics*. It is worth noting that *Politics* is thought to be a collection of Aristotle's lecture notes.[2] Scholars who accept this theory believe that *Politics* formed the basis of the lectures that he delivered to his students at his school, The Lyceum,* an "important center of secondary education in Athens"[3] where Aristotle trained the future leaders of Athens and other city-states.

Given his audience, it is not surprising that Aristotle chose to emphasize the study of real political constitutions, more or less abandoning the mode of utopian thought associated with his teacher Plato.* Aristotle was not training future philosophers; he was training future politicians and generals. The fact that *Politics* probably represents a collection of lecture notes, rather than a book that Aristotle intended to publish, also has implications for the way the work is written.

> *"So, do you think that our discussion will be any less satisfactory if we cannot demonstrate that it is possible to found a city that is the same as the one we described in speech?"*
>
> ——Plato, *The Republic*

Approach

Aristotle's aim in *Politics* is "to consider what form of political community is best of all."[4] Like his predecessors, he shared the belief that man was made good or better by living in societies governed by laws. Previous thinkers—Plato among them—theorized about "perfect states". These states did not exist; this was pure philosophy, with the objective of imagining what could be. In the text, Aristotle examines previous theories about the perfect state, but also looks at "other constitutions... such as actually exist in well-governed states."[5] In other words, Aristotle's method is more scientific—he works from the evidence to discover which constitution is the most beneficial for its citizens.

In this new approach to political philosophy, Aristotle abandons the theoretical search for an "ideal" way of doing things in favor of looking at how people can create stable political communities that benefit their citizens. He uses evidence to defend his approach. Addressing Plato's argument that all property ought to be equalized, Aristotle turns to history, citing the tale of a ruler who experimented with the edict that "the citizens of the state ought to have equal possessions".

Aristotle shows that this edict led to many men having more property than they were accustomed to, resulting in citizens "living in luxury or penury", which, in turn, caused political unrest.[6] Aristotle assesses the merit of the claim that people should have equal property on the basis of the evidence, rather than through abstract theory.

Contribution in Context

To grasp *Politics* fully, it is essential to understand the final chapters of Aristotle's work, *Nicomachean Ethics*. This was the text that first depicted humankind achieving happiness—*eudaemonia**—through the correct combination of nature, habit, and excellence.[7] According to Aristotle, people may have a deep-rooted need to be virtuous, but to realize that need they also have to practice virtuous behavior and live in an environment that supports and reinforces virtuous behavior. People who make laws "ought to stimulate men to excellence and urge them forward by the motive of the noble," he says. In other words, because most men will not choose by themselves to be noble, the state—which has laws that exist to help improve mankind—should force them to be better.[8]

Many scholars believe that the final section of the *Nicomachean Ethics* shows Aristotle making a transition from thinking about ethics to thinking about politics. There is a logical connection between *Politics* and *Ethics* because Aristotle asserts that man can become virtuous (the object of ethics), through political community and the right constitution. At the end of *Ethics*, Aristotle writes, "When [constitutions] have been studied we shall perhaps be more likely to see which constitution is best, and how each must be ordered and what laws and customs it must use."[9] This is "practical wisdom": it considers ethical issues and the *effect* of those ethical considerations. That combination of theory and practical experience was innovative, shaping the tradition of political theory.

---

1. Aristotle, "Nicomachean Ethics," 7. Book X, Chapter 9, in *The Politics and The Constitution of Athens*, ed. Stephen Everson of *Cambridge Texts in the History of Political Thought*, series editors Raymond Geuss and Quentin Skinner (Cambridge: Cambridge University Press, 1996), $1181^b/11-15$.
2. Stephen Everson, "Introduction," in *The Politics and The Constitution of Athens*, ed. Stephen Everson, *Cambridge Texts in the History of Political Thought*, series editors Raymond Geuss and Quentin Skinner (Cambridge: Cambridge University Press, 1996), X/XI.
3. John Patrick Lynch, *Aristotle's School: A Study of a Greek Educational Institution* (Berkeley: University of California Press, 1972), 46.
4. Aristotle, *Politics*, 30. Book II, Chapter 1, in *The Politics and The Constitution of Athens*, ed. Stephen Everson of *Cambridge Texts in the History of Political Thought*, series editors Raymond Geuss and Quentin Skinner (Cambridge: Cambridge University Press, 1996), 1260b/25–31.
5. Aristotle, *Politics*, 30. Book II, Chapter 1, 1260b/25–31.
6. Aristotle, *Politics*, 43–46. Book II, Chapter 7, 1266b/1–40.
7. Aristotle, *Politics*, 184–185. Book VII, Chapter 13, $1332^a/8-1332^b/10$.
8. Aristotle, "Nicomachean Ethics," 3–7. Book X, Chapter 9, 1180a/7–8.
9. Aristotle, "Nicomachean Ethics," 3–7. Book X, Chapter 9, 1181b/20–23.

SECTION 2
IDEAS

MODULE 5
MAIN IDEAS

KEY POINTS

* Aristotle said that man's natural state is living within a political society.
* He argued that political association helps people to become just and work towards their common interest.
* Scholars are still debating the way *Politics* is structured.

Key Themes

In *Politics* Aristotle has three key themes:
- Teleology.* *Telos* means "end" and, according to the principle of teleology, everything is defined by its end state. For example, a seed is defined by its purpose to become a plant. Every political community also comes together to accomplish a particular end.
- The "good life". Aristotle discusses what this is and how it might be achieved.
- The constitution* of the political community (or, roughly, the laws deciding how power is distributed). Aristotle assesses the different forms a constitution might take and which form best serves its citizens.

These three key themes fit together to produce Aristotle's overall argument: man's ultimate purpose is to become more virtuous through living within a political community. This is what he means by the famous phrase, "man is by nature a political animal."[1] A person's "natural state" is living in association with other human beings, and humanity can find happiness living in the political community. Therefore, Aristotle argues, it is natural that political communities form, and it is ethically right that a community's laws ensure the improvement of its citizens.

Aristotle discusses three different types of constitutions in *Politics*: rule by the one, rule by the few, or rule by the many. He says that each of these constitutions has a true form and a "perverted" form. When the rulers of a community aim to provide for the *polis** as a whole, then the constitution is true. When the rulers seek only their own private good, the constitution is perverted. The good constitutions are kingship (the one), aristocracy (the few), and constitutional polity (the many). The bad constitutions are tyranny (the one), oligarchy (the few), and democracy (the many). This is not an original distinction, Aristotle points out, but one Plato made that he expanded.[2]

> "Every state is a community of some kind, and every community is established with a view to some good; for everyone always acts in order to obtain that which they think good. But, if all communities aim at some good, the state or political community, which is the highest of all, and which embraces all the rest, aims at good in a greater degree than any other, and at the highest good."
>
> ——Aristotle, *Politics*

Exploring the Ideas

Aristotle introduces the concept of teleology right at the start of *Politics*, writing: "Every state is a community of some kind, and every community is established with a view to some good."[3] Aristotle gives a swift account of how political communities emerge: they begin with "natural" couplings of man and woman, master and slave, and children in "households". Several households join so that they can fulfill the "bare needs of life" more effectively.[4] As more households come together, forming a larger society, the "bare needs" of life are more than adequately fulfilled. At this point, the households continue to associate "for the sake of the good life".[5]

But what is the "good life" according to Aristotle?

It is not only that humans find satisfaction from being together, he says, but, through sharing opinions with others, people develop concepts of good and bad, justice and injustice.[6] Aristotle believes that politics, goodness, and justice are all products of human nature and human intelligence, realized through our capacity to speak to one another about our ideas. He argues, "Political society exists for the sake of noble actions." By "noble actions", Aristotle means the pursuit of justice—working together to achieve "the common interest".[7]

Politics is the means by which the "common interest" is determined. Aristotle says that social goods should be distributed in a way that favors the good of the citizens as a whole, rather than, for example, those with wealth.[8] He gives the example of a flute player, arguing that the best flute player should be given the best flute on the basis of his ability to play the flute. Politics is a mechanism by which man can incentivize people to work towards the common interest.

Language and Expression

Students of politics must keep several issues in mind when reading *Politics*.

First, *Politics* is not a stand-alone work. Aristotle discusses much of his understanding of the good life and *telos* in *Nicomachean Ethics*, and the two texts are closely related. Second, most scholars believe that Aristotle did not write *Politics* for publication. The American political scientist Carnes Lord* says that the most common assumption about Aristotle's works is that they "represent notes which served as the basis for lectures given by Aristotle to students of The Lyceum."[9]

The German classicist Werner Jaeger,* a famous scholar of Aristotle, believed that *Politics* was not even a coherent set of lecture notes. He argued that the books that make up *Politics* were cobbled together at a later date, because books IV to VI deal with Aristotle's practical notions of government in the real world, while other books (I to III and VII to VIII) are much more idea-driven.[10]

Lord disagrees with Jaeger. He thinks it is possible that *Politics* was not a set of lecture notes, but rather a reference work given to students. In this interpretation, the internal inconsistencies in the work come from student annotations and transcription errors, which would be "difficult to distinguish from earlier additions by Aristotle himself."[11] The organization and method of *Politics* is still under debate.

1. Aristotle, *Politics*, 70. Book III, Chapter 6, in *The Politics and The Constitution of Athens*, ed. Stephen Everson of *Cambridge Texts in the History of Political Thought*, series editors Raymond Geuss and Quentin Skinner (Cambridge: Cambridge University Press, 1996), $1278^b/19-20$.
2. Aristotle, *Politics*, 93. Book IV, Chapter 2, $1289^b/45-46$.
3. Aristotle, *Politics*, 11. Book I, Chapter 1, $1252^a/1-2$.
4. Aristotle, *Politics*, 12. Book I, Chapter 1, $1252^b/30$.
5. Aristotle, *Politics*, 12. Book I, Chapter 1, $1252^b/31$.
6. Aristotle, *Politics*, 14. Book I, Chapter 1, $1253^a/10-15$.
7. Aristotle, *Politics*, 76. Book III, Chapter 9, $1281^b/18$.
8. Aristotle, *Politics*, 80. Book III, Chapter 12, $1282^a/39-40$.
9. Carnes Lord, "The Character and Composition of Aristotle's *Politics*," *Political Theory* 9, No. 4 (1981): 461.
10. Werner Jaeger, *Aristotle: Fundamentals of the History of His Development*, trans. Richard Robinson, (Oxford: Oxford University Press, 1948), 283–285.
11. Lord, "The Character and Composition of Aristotle's *Politics*," 474.

MODULE 6
SECONDARY IDEAS

KEY POINTS

- According to Aristotle, a constitution* based on the middle class—meaning a state governed by the middle class—has the most realistic chance of making citizens more virtuous.
- Factionalism,* or splits in the community, along lines of wealth leads to the degeneration of the constitution of a state.
- Aristotle argues that public, universal education will help safeguard a constitution.

Other Ideas

In *Politics*, Aristotle explains why political life is important and describes how communities should be organized. "We should consider not only what form of government is best," he writes, "but also what is possible and what is easily attainable by all."[1]

How does a *polis* make improvements in the way it is organized and governed? Aristotle devotes Books IV to VIII of *Politics* to explaining how his political theories can be applied in the real world.

To comprehend Aristotle's arguments, it is vital to understand the difference between politics as an *episteme* (or a "science,") and politics as a *techne* (or "art"). In this context, "art" does not refer to a cultural form such as a painting, but rather to a trade such as carpentry or masonry. According to the British academic Stephen Everson* in his introduction to a collection of Aristotle's writings, "In possessing an art someone is capable of producing something: a doctor can produce health because he possesses the art of medicine."

So, for Aristotle, "The political scientist can produce states."[2]

Aristotle's main ideas look at the theory of what makes a good state. His secondary ideas look at how those theories may be translated into the production of real states: the art of politics.

> "The best is often unattainable, and therefore the true legislator and statesman ought to be acquainted, not only with which is best in the abstract, but also with that which is best relatively to circumstances."
>
> ——Aristotle, *Politics*

Exploring the Ideas

"What is the best constitution for most states," Aristotle asks in *Politics*, "and the best life for most men?"

He asks this question in the context of conditions that actually exist in the real world.[3] One of the factors he considers is the social mix within a city in which "one class is very rich, another very poor, and a third in [the middle]."[4] The percentage of the population that falls into each class will make each city-state very different from another. They will then have different constitutions. "Where the number of the poor exceeds a given proportion, there will naturally be a democracy," Aristotle writes, and when the wealthy gain a disproportionate amount of power, there will be an oligarchy.[5]

A disproportionate number of either poor or rich is deeply problematic, he continues. In this situation, the rich will become greedy, and the poor will become petty. Factions* will form in which people at the extremes of society develop a distorted view of justice.

From factions come revolutions and the destruction of the state.

According to Aristotle, to prevent the social distortions that occur when people seek to further their own desires and advantages above all else, the best constitution should be organized around the middle classes "for no other is free from faction." Without factions, the political community is better able to unite around the common interest.[6] The middle classes also have a balanced view of justice. They do not "covet other men's goods; or do others covet theirs." This class is able to both command and obey, but does not resent being commanded.[7]

Aristotle's ideas about a constitution based on the middle classes is neither an oligarchy* (a government ruled by a small and wealthy elite), nor a democracy* (a government led by all adult men eligible to debate and vote). It is a *polity*,* a mix between these two forms of government.

Aristotle's belief that, in the real world, the middle way is best, is prevalent throughout the book.

Overlooked

One aspect of *Politics* that scholars have often overlooked is Aristotle's discussion of education. Aristotle presents an argument for state education in Book VIII of *Politics*.[8] It is necessary for rulers to educate children, he argues, so that they learn the skills and virtues required to maintain a sound constitution. Since "the whole city has one [purpose]," he writes, "it is manifest that education should be one and the same for all, and that it should be public and not private."[9]

In the ideal society, according to Aristotle, the state would provide equal access to education to the children of all citizens. He claims that there is an important link between education and the character of the state, since "the character of democracy creates democracy, and the character of oligarchy creates oligarchy; and always the better the character, the better the government."[10] So the state can cultivate the character of its future generations by investing in their education. This system could be viewed as a means of indoctrination, ensuring that citizens do not resist the power of the state. It could also be viewed as an egalitarian and liberating proposal that guarantees a certain level of education for the state's citizens.

Recent scholars have highlighted Aristotle's discussion of education, arguing that it represents an important part of his overall thesis.[11] The Belgian academic Pierre Destrée* points out that education helps people to flourish within the state by teaching them the values of the state: "It is because we are 'political animals', that is animals who need to live in a city in order to fulfill their desire for happiness by sharing in some values and in activities that express those values, that the way to be prepared for such a life must be provided by the city we live in."[12]

---

1. Aristotle, *Politics*, 92. Book IV, Chapter 1, in *The Politics and The Constitution of Athens*, ed. Stephen Everson of *Cambridge Texts in the History of Political Thought*, series editors Raymond Geuss and Quentin Skinner (Cambridge: Cambridge University Press, 1996), 1288^b/36–38.
2. Stephen Everson, "Introduction" in *The Politics and The Constitution of Athens*, ed. Stephen Everson, *Cambridge Texts in the History of Political Thought*, series editors Raymond Geuss and Quentin Skinner (Cambridge: Cambridge University Press, 1996).

3. Aristotle, *Politics*, 92. Book IV, Chapter 1, 1294^b/25–27.
4. Aristotle, *Politics*, 107. Book IV, Chapter 11, 1295^b/1–22.
5. Aristotle, *Politics*, 109. Book IV, Chapter 12, 1296^b/24–27.
6. Aristotle, *Politics*, 108. Book IV, Chapter 11, 1296^a/7.
7. Aristotle, *Politics*, 108, Book IV, Chapter 11, 1295^b/29–30.
8. Aristotle, *Politics*, 195–207. Book VIII.
9. Aristotle, *Politics*, 195. Book VIII, Chapter 1, 1337^a/21–23.
10. Aristotle, *Politics*, 195. Book VIII, Chapter 1, 1337^a/16–18.
11. Pierre Destrée, "Education, Leisure and Politics" in *The Cambridge Companion to* Aristotle's *Politics*, eds. Marguerite Deslauriers and Pierre Destrée (Cambridge and New York: Cambridge University Press, 2013), 301–323.
12. Destrée, "Education", 306.

MODULE 7
ACHIEVEMENT

KEY POINTS

* Although Aristotle's *Politics* has inspired many political thinkers, people have criticized it because he does not offer details about how to realize all his ideas.
* Aristotle was a prominent teacher and intellectual in Athens.
* Aristotle's argument for "natural slavery" has made some modern readers uncomfortable with the work. However, other interpreters believe Aristotle was actually condemning slavery.

Assessing the Argument

In *Politics*, Aristotle presents his vision of the best possible political structure within the constraints of the real world. His intention was to work out how people could be improved by life within the community—and in some ways, he achieves this. Aristotle articulates a number of core points: what the aim of a society should be, what kinds of societies there are, and which kind of society is best at improving the lives of its citizens.

However, some thinkers believe *Politics* is an unfinished work. Aristotle's explanation of how the state is to be arranged lacks a detailed description of one important element: the education system.

Dorothea Frede,* a professor of philosophy at the University of California, notes that Aristotle's "plan for the citizen's education unfortunately is not carried out beyond the blueprint for the musical education of children."[1] Frede suggests two possible explanations for this. It is possible that certain aspects of a more complete work were lost. Aristotle could also have decided not to carry out a project of such size. It would be a nearly, it not totally, impossible task to list all of the factors that make for a successful education system.

> "Aristotle's theory of natural slavery is at least potentially a critical theory. A slave owner who pondered it seriously would have to ask himself: 'Is my slave really a natural slave? Or is he too shrewd and purposeful?'"
>
> ——Malcolm Schofield, *"Ideology and Philosophy in Aristotle's Theory of Slavery"*

Achievement in Context

If, as is widely believed, Aristotle's work *Politics* was created from reconstructed lectures that he delivered at his school, The Lyceum,* that indicates the impact Aristotle's teaching had during his lifetime. It is unlikely that his lecture notes would have been retained if he had not been intellectually influential.

The Peripatetic ("walking") scholars, named perhaps for Aristotle's style of pacing around as he taught, preserved Aristotle's work. The Lyceum and the peripatetic tradition remained important after Aristotle's death, as his students continued his work. The American historian David C. Lindberg* describes how, on Aristotle's death, Theophrastus,* a close associate of the philosopher "assumed the headship of The Lyceum."[2]

Although Theophrastus continued Aristotle's program of research, his only surviving works focus on botany and geology. The texts in the library of The Lyceum, including Aristotle's writings, were bequeathed to notable scholars around the Mediterranean, eventually ending up in the hands of the Greek philosopher Andronicus of Rhodes* who "arranged and edited them, bringing them into prominence and wider circulation."[3] In the twelfth century, William of Moerbeke,* a Flemish philosopher and monk from what today is the Netherlands, translated *Politics* into Latin. That brought Aristotle's ideas to a wider audience, which recognized their significance immediately.

Although many aspects of Aristotle's wider philosophy aroused mistrust in the Roman Catholic Church, the intellectual tradition known as Scholasticism*—which was concerned with collecting, preserving and using the wisdom of the past—helped to reconcile Aristotelian thought with Catholic doctrine.

Limitations

One key aspect of Aristotle's *Politics* has been particularly off-putting to modern readers: his defense of the institution of slavery and his idea that some people are "natural slaves". According to Aristotle, "that which can foresee by the exercise of mind is by nature lord and master," and he who can carry out what his master foresees is "by nature a slave."[4]

Aristotle believes this arrangement is mutually beneficial since masters and slaves share the same goals. However, the "natural master" cannot carry out all his plans on his own, and the "natural slave" is not capable of independent planning—he has to be directed to act. Aristotle does, however, argue against slavery by "convention". He says that the practice in which a rational human being is made a slave simply because he or she has had the misfortune of being captured should not be allowed.[5] This is not a mutually beneficial relationship.

Some scholars, notably the British classicist Malcolm Schofield,* believe that Aristotle may have been subtly making a case *against* slavery. Schofield points out that, in criticizing slavery "by convention" (through capturing people) Aristotle argues that the vast majority of humanity should be excluded from slavery. After all, how many people are incapable of thought? Schofield suggests that Aristotle may have written his chapters on slavery to force "a slave owner [to] ask himself:'Is my slave really a natural slave? Or is he too shrewd and purposeful?'"[6] So it is important to interpret Aristotle's ideas about slavery carefully. It may be that they contain an implicit criticism of the "unethical" practice of the slavery common at Aristotle's time.

---

1. Dorothea Frede, "The Political Character of Aristotle's Ethics," in *The Cambridge Companion to Aristotle's Politics* (Cambridge: Cambridge University Press, 2013), 33.
2. David C. Lindberg, *The Beginnings of Western Science: The European Scientific Tradition in Philosophical, Religious, and Institutional Context, Prehistory to AD 1450* (Chicago: University of Chicago, 2008), 73.
3. Lindberg, *The Beginnings of Western Science*, 74.
4. Aristotle, *Politics*, 12. Book 1, Chapter 1 in *The Politics and The Constitution of Athens*, ed. Stephen Everson of *Cambridge Texts in the History of Political Thought*, series editors Raymond Geuss and Quentin Skinner (Cambridge: Cambridge University Press, 1996), $1252^a/31-34$.
5. Aristotle, *Politics*, 19. Book 1, Chapter 7, $1255^b/12-14$.
6. Malcolm Schofield, "Ideology and Philosophy in Aristotle's Theory of Slavery," in *Aristotle's Politics: Critical Essays*, ed. Richard Kraut and Steven Skultety (Lanham: Rowman and Littlefield, 2005), 100.

MODULE 8
PLACE IN THE AUTHOR'S WORK

KEY POINTS

- Some thinkers argue that *Politics* was composed at two different times since the early books are more "Platonist" (more obviously bearing the influence of Aristotle's teacher Plato) than the middle books.
- Aristotle used the same analytical approach to every subject he wrote about. He would break down the basic principles of an art or science in order to find its core meaning.
- Aristotle also wrote across many disciplines, including poetics, physics, and natural science. His work in all these disciplines has been extremely influential.

Positioning

Different sections of Aristotle's *Politics* may have been composed at the different times. As a result, it is hard to assess what position this work holds in relation to Aristotle's other writing.

Aristotle wrote his early work while he was still under the influence of the ideas of his teacher Plato.* These pieces contain more Platonic concepts than Aristotle's later work. The British academic Thomas Case* explained Plato's doctrine as viewing all existence as reflecting perfect, supernatural "forms". So tables are only "tables" because they resemble the "ideal form" of a perfect, theoretical table.

Aristotle, in contrast, holds that all things are separate. Tables are not all reflections of a perfect, supernatural table. They are understood to be tables because they possess individual qualities that make them more table-like than chair-like.[1] Some thinkers—notably the German classicist Werner Jaeger*—have concluded that Aristotle began his intellectual life as a Platonist* but became more "Aristotelian" as he developed into a more established thinker in his own right.[2]

Some of the books that make up *Politics* offer a Platonic theory of political ideals (books I to III and books VII to VIII), while others display an Aristotelian commitment to the study of individual constitutions (books IV to VI). Scholars still debate whether Aristotle wrote *Politics* early or late in his career, or whether the book straddles both periods of his life.

> "Politics *is to be ranked amongst the greatest works of political philosophy."*
>
> —— Stephen Everson, "Introduction," in *Politics*

Integration

Aristotle's intellectual life was not focused purely on politics; he was a broad-ranging scholar who inquired into logic, science, rhetoric,* and even poetry. Aristotle's approach to these subjects, however, was consistently analytical and methodical; he broke down whatever he was studying into its fundamental parts. He then used this knowledge of the fundamental building blocks of a discipline to study how it emerged and the best way that it could develop.

Aristotle opens his *Poetics*, for example: "We are to discuss both poetry in general and the capacity of each of its genres; the canons of plot construction needed for poetic excellence; also the number and character of poetry's components... beginning, as is natural, from first principles."[3] He seeks to understand the distinct parts of poetry, what makes poetry excellent, and how poetry can become excellent.

His investigation into animals proceeds in a similarly analytical way. "Of the parts of animals some are simple: to wit, all such as divide into parts uniform with themselves, as flesh unto flesh," he writes. Others divide into distinct parts so that "the hand does not divide into hands nor the face into faces."[4] Aristotle breaks the complexity of animal life down into parts: hands are made of palms, fingers, and below this, cells. This methodical approach is thought of as distinctively Aristotelian.

Significance

"*Politics*," writes the British academic Stephen Everson,* "is to be ranked amongst the greatest works of political philosophy."[5] Yet Aristotle's other works also had a seminal influence on different disciplines. For example, his ideas about physics dominated Western science until the seventeenth century. And the Italian historian Stefano Perfetti* describes how Aristotle's work on zoology* was admired during the medieval period. "Halfway through the thirteenth century, we already find the entire corpus of Aristotle's natural writings" prescribed to students at the University of Padua, in what is now northern Italy.[6]

Although later scholarship superseded some of Aristotle's concepts, this is not necessarily true of *Politics*. Readers now criticize some sections of this work, such as its problematic sections on natural slavery and the role of women in society. But the core message of Aristotle's *Politics* remains at the heart of a flourishing contemporary political theory: that political affiliation can improve peoples' lives.

In the modern world, Aristotle has become a source of wisdom for a range of famous scholars including the Indian economist and Nobel laureate Amartya Sen,* the American philosopher Martha Nussbaum,* and even the American political philosopher Michael Sandel,* who is famous for his theories about justice and community.

---

1. Thomas Case, "Aristotle," *Aristotle's Philosophical Development: Problems and Prospects*, ed. William Robert Wians (London: Rowman and Littlefield, 1990), 1–2.
2. Daniel Graham, *Aristotle's Two Systems* (Oxford: Oxford University Press, 1990), 5.
3. Aristotle, *Poetics*, 1, Book 1, translated by Richard Janko (Indianapolis: Hackett Publishing, 1987), $47^a/1-2$.
4. Aristotle, *History of the Animals*, (Adelaide: University of Adelaide), ebook. https://ebooks.adelaide.edu.au/a/aristotle/history/book1.html.
5. Stephen Everson, "Introduction" in *The Politics and The Constitution of Athens*, ed. Stephen Everson, *Cambridge Texts in the History of Political Thought*, series editors Raymond Geuss and Quentin Skinner (Cambridge: Cambridge University Press, 1996), 1.
6. Stefano Perfetti, *Aristotle's Zoology and its Renaissance Commentators* (Leuven: Leuven University Press, 2000), 1.

SECTION 3
IMPACT

MODULE 9
THE FIRST RESPONSES

KEY POINTS

* The earliest criticisms of *Politics* focused on Aristotle's overly careful, formal approach.
* *Politics* was treated as an authoritative source of political fact through the European Middle Ages* (roughly the fifth to the fifteenth century) and numerous scholars composed commentaries on it.
* By the early modern period,* which began around the end of the fifteenth century, scholars were less willing to accept Aristotle as authoritative. While they shared his interests, they wanted to gather their own evidence.

Criticism

Aristotle's *Politics* was probably not printed for wide distribution. As a result, people did not respond to it in any serious way until much later.

When Western thinkers rediscovered *Politics* in the thirteenth century, it had "far reaching consequences for political thought."¹ But although Aristotle's ideas inspired many Christian medieval scholars, *Politics* also provoked some criticism.

The Italian humanist* scholar Petrarch,* for example, argued that Aristotle's approach to politics is too careful and systematic. He took issue with Aristotle's notion that men can become noble simply by understanding what nobility is, rather than by being passionate about virtue. For Petrarch, political life is an emotional process; Aristotle was too calm.

"Aristotle explains what virtue* is," he writes, "but reading his works does not offer... words that set on fire the heart and make it love virtue and detest vice."[2] Petrarch recognized the importance of Aristotle's thought, however. He considered himself obliged to find a position that reconciled the worldly and rational Aristotelian idea of the "good life" with the Christian idea that a life should be valued by the nature of our relationship to the divine.

Whereas Aristotle described "the good life" in terms of human fulfillment in the world, for Petrarch, life without love for a personal God—an idea connected to emotion and joy—could not be perfectly described as "good".

Other thinkers, among them the Italian intellectual St Thomas Aquinas,* resolved this by arguing that wisdom could be found in many places. The key for Aquinas was to harvest that wisdom through study.

> "Let them keep their exorbitant opinion of everything that regards them, and the naked name Aristotle which delights many ignorant people by its four syllables. Moreover, let them have the vain joy and the unfounded elation which is so near to ruin; in short, let them have all the profit people who are ignorant and puffed up earn from their errors in vague and easy credulity."
>
> —— Petrarch, *On His Own Ignorance*

Responses

The earliest comprehensive criticism of *Politics* that we have was produced around a thousand years after Aristotle's death. He was, therefore, unable to respond to it. Many thinkers appreciated, rather than criticized, Aristotle's ideas. When his work was rediscovered in the medieval period, scholars updated *Politics*, adapting it to the new political structures of the day. This was a tacit way of showing admiration for Aristotle's work, despite the fact that he "was without the light of Christian revelation, and without the medieval conception of the church in society."³

In the medieval period, a movement called Scholasticism* dominated western intellectual thought. The aim of Scholasticism was to understand, and benefit from, all accessible sources of wisdom—rediscovered classical texts and the *Bible* alike. This movement arose in large part due to the desire of medieval scholars to reconcile Aristotelian thought with Catholic doctrine. Prominent thinkers in the Scholastic tradition, notably Aquinas, published commentaries on Aristotle's *Politics*—going through the text line by line to reveal the philosopher's insights.⁴

Aquinas's most famous work is *Summa Theologica*, which discusses the teachings of the Roman Catholic Church. Its primary goal was to unite worldly concerns like politics with issues of theology.* Aquinas cites Aristotle in *Summa*, despite the fact that Aristotle was not a Christian. Aquinas respectfully refers to Aristotle as "the Philosopher" and endorses many of his ideas. Quoting Aristotle's *Ethics*, for example, Aquinas writes: "The Philosopher says happiness is an operation according to perfect virtue."⁵ Moreover, Aquinas argued, "The proper effect of the law is to lead its subjects to their proper virtue,"* thereby improving the character of those who obey the law.6

Conflict and Consensus

By the early modern period, attitudes towards Aristotle had begun to change. Although thinkers still considered his ideas inspirational, they were starting to use his methods to draw their own conclusions about the world. Writing about the early modern period, the British academic Ernest Barker* discussed the impact of Aristotelian thought on Niccolò Machiavelli,* a Florentine diplomat and political theorist who has been called the inventor of modern political theory and who was, says Barker,"nurtured upon Aristotle from birth."7 According to Barker, Machiavelli used Aristotle's classification of constitutions: rule by one, rule by the few, or rule by many.

Both thinkers were interested in understanding how tyrants preserve their power. Writing of tyranny—the "perverted" form of kingship—Aristotle says, "Though power must be retained as the foundation in all else the tyrant should act or appear to act in the character of a king." In other words, the tyrant should appear to act as a ruler who cares for the common interests of his subjects.8 Those words mirror Machiavelli's famous advice that "a ruler who succeeds in creating [a generous] image of himself will enjoy a fine reputation."9

However, Barker also argues that Machiavelli "cannot be said to be indebted to Aristotle." Unlike the medieval commentators, "he does not lay down general principles from Aristotle" as though they are authoritative, but rather "collects the facts of the present" and draws his own conclusions.10 Moreover, Machiavelli rejects the link between morality and politics. Aristotle believed that the ultimate end of politics was to improve the lives of citizens. For Machiavelli, politics was just a way of achieving power. Aristotle rejected Plato's* idealism in favor of greater empiricism.* In the same way, Machiavelli rejected Aristotle.

---

1. Christopher Kleinherz, ed., "Aristotle and Aristotelianism," *Medieval Italy: An Encyclopedia*, (Oxford: Routledge, 2004), 56.
2. Petrarch, quoted in Christopher Kleinhenz, *Medieval Italy: An Encyclopedia Volume I A-K* (Oxford: Routledge, 2004), 117.
3. Conor Martin, "Some Medieval Commentaries on Aristotle's *Politics*," *History* 36 (1951): 34.
4. St. Thomas Aquinas, *Commentary on Aristotle's Politics*, translated by Richard J. Regan (Indianapolis: Hackett), 2007.
5. St. Thomas Aquinas, *Summa Theologica*, (Mobilereference: 2010), 1867.
6. Aquinas, *Summa Theologica*, 3108.
7. Sir Ernest Barker, *The Political Thought of Plato and Aristotle* (New York: Dover Publications, 1959), 515.
8. Aristotle, *Politics*, 148. Book 5, Chapter 11 in *The Politics and The Constitution of Athens*, ed. Stephen Everson of *Cambridge Texts in the History of Political Thought*, series editors Raymond Geuss and Quentin Skinner (Cambridge: Cambridge University Press, 1996), $1314^a/39-40$.
9. Niccolò Machiavelli, *The Prince*, ed. Quentin Skinner and Russell Price (Cambridge: Cambridge University Press, 1988), 63.
10. Barker, *The Political Thought of Plato and Aristotle*, 517.

MODULE 10
THE EVOLVING DEBATE

KEY POINTS

* One of Aristotle's key ideas was called political naturalism: * the idea that it is natural for humans to live in the *polis*.* This aspect of his thought was reinvigorated in the eighteenth century by thinkers like the conservative Irish statesman Edmund Burke.*
* *Politics* inspired the modern school of thought known as virtue ethics.*
* The American philosopher Martha Nussbaum* applies virtue ethics to politics. She suggests that political communities should aim to develop the virtues of their citizens.

Uses and Problems

Aristotle's *Politics* had an enormous effect on medieval political philosophy. The Scottish philosopher J. H. Burns* writes, "The translation of Aristotle's *Politics* and *Nicomachean Ethics* was crucial" for the political thought of the thirteenth century.[1]

By the early modern period,* political thinking had changed. Aristotle believed that politics could lift the citizens of a *polis* out of "mere life," helping them to achieve "the good life." But during the early modern period,* from around the sixteenth to the eighteenth centuries, the political philosophy known as liberalism* started to gain influence. Grounded in ideas about individual freedom and equality, liberalism argued that the role of the state was to enable individual liberty, rather than to improve its citizens. The English political philosopher Thomas Hobbes* famously criticized *Politics* for just this reason, saying, "Scarce anything can be... more repugnant to government than much of that he hath said in *Politics*."² Hobbes believed that the state existed to provide—exclusively—for the "mere life" of its citizens.

Liberalism,* however, had its critics, who shared some of Aristotle's ideas. In 1791, the Irish statesman Edmund Burke wrote his now-famous *Reflections on the Revolution in France*. In it, he criticized the liberal ideas that underpinned the democratic French Revolution,* noting, "Aristotle observes... that a democracy has many striking points of resemblance with a tyranny."³ Burke also shared Aristotle's belief that political association, with power distributed properly, will ultimately improve all those who participate in it. "Whenever man is put over men, as the better nature ought ever to preside, in that case more particularly, he should as nearly as possible be approximated to his perfection."⁴

> *"If I recollect rightly, Aristotle observes that a democracy has many striking points of resemblance with a tyranny. Of this I am certain, that in a democracy, the majority of the citizens is capable of exercising the most cruel oppressions upon the minority."*
>
> —— Edmund Burke, *Reflections on the Revolution in France*

Schools of Thought

Today, Aristotle's ethical and political thought is one of the key inspirations for virtue ethics, a movement in philosophy concerned with the moral principles governing an individual's actions. Other approaches to ethics include deontology,* which is concerned with the rules an individual follows and consequentialism,* which focuses on the consequences of an individual's actions.

The field of virtue ethics emphasizes the virtues. If there were a debate as to whether a drowning person should be saved, then "a virtue ethicist will emphasize the fact that helping the person would be charitable or benevolent."[5] They would also argue that it is good—virtuous—for people to be charitable or benevolent.

The British philosopher G. E. M. Anscombe* was one of the discipline's most important thinkers. Her article "Modern Moral Philosophy," first published in 1958, helped to embed modern virtue ethics as a distinctive line of inquiry.[6] Anscombe and the other virtue ethicists are primarily interested in Aristotle's *Ethics* rather than *Politics*. They use the idea of acting virtuously (developing oneself) as an alternative to acting "morally" (following the instructions of a lawmaker). Anscombe argued that ethical actions are ethical not because they follow some set of given *rules*, but instead because they are in accordance with a set of *virtues*.

In Current Scholarship

Virtue ethics can be applied to real-world politics. Referring to ethical theories too abstract to be useful in the real world, the American philosopher Martha Nussbaum* writes, "From many different sides one hears of a disaffection with ethical theories that are remote from concrete human experience."

One of the first to apply virtue ethics to modern political theory, Nussbaum goes on to say that Aristotle "was not only the defender of an ethical theory based on the virtues, but also the defender of a single objective account of the human good."[7] Some thinkers claim that what is good varies from person to person. Nussbaum argues that Aristotle believed in a state of being that was beneficial to all human beings—"the good life"—which people could achieve by developing their virtues. Aristotle also described the virtues that they needed to develop, providing an ethical guide to human existence that can be applied in the real world. His ideas can be used to improve key areas of human endeavor like education or law-making.

Nussbaum herself provides "a sketch for an objective human morality based upon the idea of virtuous action—that is, of appropriate functioning in each human sphere."[8] In other words, she presents an overview of ethics based on an objective idea of what is good for humanity, such as the development of virtues like courage, kindness, and generosity.

---

1. J.H. Burns, "Introduction: Politics, Institutions, and Ideas," in *The Cambridge History of Medieval Political Thought* (Cambridge: Cambridge University Press, 1988), 356.
2. Thomas Hobbes, *Leviathan*, ed. J.C.A. Gaskin (Oxford: Oxford University Press, 1998), 143, 445.
3. Edmund Burke, *Reflections on the Revolution in France* (New Haven: Yale University Press, 2003), 106.
4. Burke, *Reflections*, 79.
5. Rosalind Hursthouse, *On Virtue Ethics* (Oxford: Oxford University Press, 1999), 1.
6. G. E. M. Anscombe, "Modern Moral Philosophy," *Philosophy* 33, No. 124 (1958), 1–19.
7. Martha Nussbaum, "Non-Relative Virtues: An Aristotelian Approach," *Midwest Studies in Philosophy XIII* (1988), 33.
8. Nussbaum, "Non-Relative Virtues," 39.

MODULE 11
IMPACT AND INFLUENCE TODAY

KEY POINTS

* Aristotle is honored today as the founder of political science as a distinct discipline.
* The idea that political communities ought to improve the lives of those who live in them has become central to the capability approach* to development, according to which "development" should mean more than simply an increase in a country's income.
* Some thinkers believe the "capabilities" developed by the capability approach are too "Western." They say that it is not possible to make objective lists of virtues.

Position

The German American political philosopher Leo Strauss* highlighted the importance of Aristotle's *Politics* in the modern world, writing:"Aristotle is truly the founder of political science."[1] Aristotle was among the first thinkers to study politics by considering real-world examples and applications rather than pure ideas alone.

In her book *A Democracy of Distinction: Aristotle and the Work of Politics*, the American political scientist Jill Frank* writes that it is tempting to dismiss an ancient philosopher as "irrelevant for our times," given the scale and complexity of modern states. But Frank argues that to do so would be a mistake.[2] She also says that it would be unwise to dismiss Aristotle on the grounds of his "politics of exclusion." By this, she means Aristotle's apparent advocacy of inequality between women and men or "masters" and "slaves." It is important to look carefully at what Aristotle actually says, she writes, as "closer look opens possibilities [for modern readers] that he is usually seen to be foreclosing." She points out that there has been increasing interest in Aristotle as a source of political insight since the latter half of the twentieth century: "Scholars with varying and often opposing political commitments claim that Aristotle's writings offer rich resources for contemporary politics." [3]

Some, like Strauss, claim that Aristotle offers a justification for a politics based on rule by the "best". Others, such as Frank's colleague, the American philosopher Martha Nussbaum,* argue that Aristotle's focus on education provides "the basis for a well-functioning liberal or social democratic regime."[4] Aristotle is seen as a source of timeless political insight, even between those who may disagree about other things.

> *"If we have reasons to want more wealth, we have to ask: what precisely are these reasons, how do they work, on what are they contingent, and what are the things we can 'do' with more wealth?... Income and wealth are [not] desirable for their own sake, but because, typically, they are admirable general-purpose means for having more freedom to lead the kind of lives we have reason to value."*
>
> ——Amartya Sen, *Development as Freedom*

Interaction

Aristotle's work inspired Martha Nussbaum's view of virtue ethics.* In turn, virtue ethics stimulated a powerful theory of economic development: the "capability approach."

Championed by the Nobel Prize*-winning Indian economist Amartya Sen,* the Capability Approach states that final aim of development should be "a process of expanding the real freedoms that people enjoy."[5] Sen means that development should not simply make a country richer. Countries can be rich but also restrict their citizens' freedoms, giving them no access to political participation, healthcare, or nutrition. The Capability Approach says the goal of economic development should be to improve the lives of the people who experience that development.

This theory challenged an existing concept of development. In 1990, the British economist John Williamson* wrote an essay called, "What Washington Means By Policy Reform." In it he detailed 10 policy instruments that America used to set policy conditions when giving aid to developing countries.[6] These included:

- Market liberalization
- Increased spending in health and education
- Deficit reduction

These policies, which focused on "the standard economic objectives of growth, low inflation, a visible balance of payments, and an equitable income distribution," became known as the Washington Consensus.* This approach to economics prioritizes economic performance without articulating what that economic performance is *for*, other than the basic preservation of life.[7] That stands in clear contrast to the capability approach, which saw economic performance as a means of developing a country's citizens.

The United Nations Development Program (UNDP)* now uses the capability approach to economics. Instead of emphasizing the Gross National Product (GNP)* of a developing country, it looks at its Human Development Index (HDI).* This measures a combination of the adult literacy rate, average lifespan, and GNP per capita.[8] In other words, Aristotle inspired a concept that now lies at the heart of economic development.

The Continuing Debate

The Capability Approach has been criticized. Some thinkers have emphasized that it is problematic to assume that everyone desires certain universal freedoms, regardless of cultural context.

Although the British academic David Clark* supports the capability approach,* he takes issue with the way it is supposed to work. He asks, for example, which capabilities should the capability approach foster? His argument is that Sen's ideas are too open-ended since he has avoided detailing an objective list of the capabilities that development should bring.

In contrast, the American philosopher Martha Nussbaum,* who specifies a list based on Aristotelian virtue, may be problematic in a different way—her approach may be too high-handed. "Perhaps the only reasonable way of arriving at such a list is to consult the poor themselves," Clark writes. His point is that if we do not, we will have an idea of development that is supposed to be universal, but is in fact based on Western ideas of what it means to live a good life.[9]

Clark provides an example. A survey of South Africans indicated that their concept of the good life involves "jobs, housing, education, income, family and friends, religion, health, good clothes, recreation and relaxation, [and] safety and economic security."[10] Nussbaum, on the other hand, had proposed, "health; bodily health; bodily integrity; senses, imagination, and thought; emotions; practical reason;*affiliation; other species; play; control over one's environment, both political and material."[11]

The South African interviewees' list is more about work and relationships, whereas Nussbaum's focuses more on the development of the self.

---

1. Leo Strauss, *The City and Man* (Chicago: University of Chicago Press, 1964), 21.
2. Jill Frank, *A Democracy of Distinction: Aristotle and the Work of Politics* (Chicago: University of Chicago Press, 2005), 4.
3. Frank, *A Democracy of Distinction*, 4.
4. Frank, *A Democracy of Distinction*, 5–6.
5. Amartya Sen, *Development as Freedom* (New York: Alfred A. Knopf, 1999), 3.
6. John Williamson, *Latin American Adjustment: How Much Has Happened?* Accessed March 1, 2014 http: //faculty.washington.edu/acs22/SinklerSite/PS%20322/What%20Washington%20Means%20by%20Policy%20Reform.pdf.
7. Williamson, *Latin American Adjustment*, March 1, 2014.
8. United Nations, "Human Development Reports," Accessed Feb 25, 2014, http: //hdr.undp.org/en/statistics/hdi.
9. David Clark, *Visions of Development: A Study of Human Values* (Cheltenham: Edward Elgar, 2002), 27.
10. David Clark, "Capability Approach," in *The Elgar Companion to Development Studies* ed. David Clark (Cheltenham: Edward Elgar Publishing Limited, 2006), 38.
11. Martha Nussbaum, *Women and Human Development: The Capabilities Approach* (Cambridge: Cambridge University Press, 2000), 78–80.

MODULE 12
WHERE NEXT?

KEY POINTS

- Aristotle's overall project—to provide an account of politics centered on human improvement—continues to be an important approach.
- The American political philosopher Michael Sandel* applies Aristotle's method to the debate on same-sex marriage, saying that we should legislate according to the virtues that ought to be encouraged.
- Aristotle's *Politics* has inspired thinkers since the Middle Ages▲ and continues to do so.

Potential

The ideas that Aristotle expressed in his work *Politics* have not only inspired the capability approach to economic development, but also other thinkers who have attempted to apply his political thinking to the modern world.

The American academic Fred D. Miller Jr.,* for example, has argued that modern statesmen should "keep in view Aristotle's suggestions for practical politics."[1] In other words, politicians should keep Aristotle's idea of the "mixed" constitution in mind if we are to avoid pure populist* democracy and oligarchy.

With an echo of Aristotle, he points out that even if modern states distribute political rights among all citizens, economic power tends to concentrate in the hands of the few. Although modern states enjoy a "political order... subject to representative democratic rule... economic order is largely the result of decisions by [a few individuals with economic power]."[2]

Other thinkers, among them the American philosopher Martha Nussbaum,* highlight other aspects of *Politics* that remain relevant today. The idea of the ultimate aim of political association—the achievement of happiness through political structures—would be one.

Aristotle's book remains a source of inspiration for political thinkers from across the political spectrum. His ideas resonate particularly with those who emphasize balance, stability, and human development.

> *"The virtues are attracting increasing interest in contemporary philosophical debate. From many different sides one hears of a dissatisfaction with ethical theories that are remote from concrete human experience."*
>
> —— Martha Nussbaum, "Non-Relative Virtues: An Aristotelian Approach"

Future Directions

The American political philosopher Michael Sandel* has updated Aristotle's ideas for the modern world. Describing his Aristotelian vision of justice in politics, he writes that "justice has something to do honoring, recognizing, promoting, and cultivating virtues and goods implicit in social practices."[3]

Like Aristotle, he argues that if we are to define something, it is vital to understand the ultimate purpose of the thing being described. So to define "rights," it's vital to know exactly what those rights are for. Another key Aristotelian aspect of Sandel's philosophy is that "justice is honorific." To create laws and administer justice, people need to understand "what virtues the social practice should honor and reward."[4] Sandel restates Aristotle's example of the distribution of flutes among flute players. The best flute players should get the best flutes, since "the purpose of flutes is to produce excellent music."[5]

In another example, Sandel addresses the debate over same-sex marriage. Some thinkers say that, in this instance, a principle of non-discrimination should apply to marriage generally. Taken to its logical extreme, however, would this not endorse marriage between any two entities—between members of the same immediate family or between people and objects? Sandel resolves this by arguing that we should ask, "Which interpretation of marriage celebrates virtues worth honoring?"

He cites the decision in favor of same-sex marriage by the South-African born Justice Margaret Marshall,* who argued that disallowing same-sex marriage "confers an official stamp of approval" on destructive stereotypes about same-sex marriage, when they are in fact worthy of the same official respect as heterosexual relationships.[6]

Sandel, in other words, shows that Aristotelian reasoning can help to solve seemingly intractable debates in modern society. The key is to ask what rights or privileges we are trying to distribute, and why.

Summary

Aristotle's *Politics* was dazzlingly original. Moreover, as an early work of empirical* analysis, it was groundbreaking. And it contains a wealth of reflections, distinctions, principles, and concepts that still have significance for political theory today. These include the notion of what constitutes "a good life" and the debate about how much the state should be involved in providing for its citizens.

Although *Politics* was overlooked for some time in the ancient world, its reappraisal by thinkers in the Middle Ages* secured its place in the history of political thought. And, in recent decades, its popularity has increased. Aristotelian ideas have inspired modern scholars like the American political philosopher Michael Sandel, the Indian economist Amartya Sen, and the American philosopher Martha Nussbaum. These thinkers question how society should function in order to provide the best possible lives for their citizens. Their work has ensured that the *Politics* will remain current.

For students of the history of political thought, the book remains enormously important as both a work of political theory and an historical account of the political climate of Ancient Greece. Most important, however, *Politics* is the book that won Aristotle his title as the world's first political scientist.

---

1. Fred D. Miller Jr., "Aristotelian Statecraft and Modern Politics," *Aristotle's Politics Today*, ed. Lenn E. Goodman and Robert B. Talisse (Albany: State University of New York Press, 2008), 30.
2. Miller, "Aristotelian Statecraft and Modern Politics," 30.
3. Michael Sandel, "Justice: What's the Right Thing to Do?" *Boston University Law Review* 91 (2011): 1303.
4. Sandel, "Justice: What's the Right Thing to Do?" 1303.
5. Sandel, "Justice: What's the Right Thing to Do?" 1304.
6. Sandel, "Justice: What's the Right Thing to Do?" 1307–1309.

GLOSSARY OF TERMS

1. **Academy (387 – 86 B.C.E.):** an elite club of scholars and young Athenian notables founded by Plato.

2. **Aristocracy:** literally, "rule by the best": government by a small number of people who merit the position and will, therefore, according to Aristotle, rule without being over-concerned with matters such as wealth.

3. **Callipolis:** name given to the "perfect" city in Plato's *Republic*. Its English translation is roughly "Beautiful City."

4. **Capability Approach:** theory of economic development that holds that we should define successful economic development by the degree to which individuals are enabled to do what they have reason to want to do.

5. **Classical Era (510 – 323 B.C.E.):** period in Greek History that saw the flowering of art, culture, and philosophy for which Ancient Greece is now famous.

6. **Consequentialism:** theoretical approach to ethics according to which an action should be judged "right" or "wrong" according to the consequences of that action.

7. **Constitution:** for Aristotle, the laws determining who holds power within a society.

8. **Democracy:** literally, "rule by the people"; for Aristotle, democracy was undesirable, since the masses would rule in their own interests—over-taxing the wealthy, for example, at the expense of a cohesive society.

9. **Deontology:** theoretical approach to ethics according to which the morality of action should be judged based on whether or not it is performed in adherence to rules or out of duty.

10. **Distributive justice:** the "just" distribution of goods in a society.

11. **Early Modern:** usually held to be the period between the end of the Middle Ages and the beginning of industrialization, around the late fifteenth century to the mid-eighteenth century.

12. **Empiricism:** theory that all knowledge is based entirely on sensed evidence as opposed to pure reason.

13. **Ethics:** moral principles that govern human behavior with regard to one another.

14. **Eudaemonia:** Greek word that means good ("eu") spirit ("daimon"); often thought of as meaning "happiness," the term is better understood to signify the idea of "human flourishing."

15. **Faction:** small group of people inside a larger community.

16. **Factionalism:** the split into "factions" (self-interested groups) of a community or society, often used with connotations of disagreement and friction.

17. **French Revolution (1789 – 99):** decade of intense political upheaval in France, in which revolutionaries experimented with a variety of different regimes—including a constitutional monarchy, a revolutionary dictatorship, a popular direct democracy, and a liberal republic—before ending with the military dictatorship of Napoleon Bonaparte.

18. **Gross National Product (GNP):** the combined value of everything, including goods and services, that citizens of a country produce—even outside that country's borders.

19. **Hellenistic Age:** period during which Ancient Greek cultural influence was at its peak, usually held to be the time between the death of Alexander the Great* in 323 B.C.E. and the emergence of the Roman Empire.

20. **Hellenistic Empire (359 – 323 B.C.E.):** group of Greek city-states that Philip II of Macedon brought under his direct control starting in 359 B.C.E. In 333 B.C.E., his son Alexander extended the empire eastward to modern-day India. Upon his death in 323 B.C.E., the empire splintered among his heirs.

21. **Human Development Index (HDI):** composite index that shows a country's overall state of "human development" by presenting life expectancy,

education, and wealth as a single number.

22. **Humanism:** a Renaissance cultural movement that emphasized study of classical literature.

23. **Liberalism:** political philosophy founded on ideas about individual freedom and equality.

24. **The Lyceum School:** school established by Aristotle in an area of Athens where people would meet called the Lyceum.

25. **Middle Ages:** period of European history that starts with the fall of Rome and ends with the Italian Renaissance (roughly from the fifth to the fifteenth century).

26. **Monarchy:** a form of government where supremacy lies with a single, usually hereditary, figure, such as a king or queen.

27. **Nobel Prize:** international award that recognizes achievement in many academic fields as well as the promotion of world peace. It is often considered one of the highest honors in the world.

28. **Oligarchy:** literally, "rule by the few." For Aristotle, an oligarchy was government by a small number of rich men—a poor system of government, since they would govern in their own interests and disregard the poor at the expense of social cohesion.

29. **Olympians:** the gods of ancient Greece. The gods were anthropomorphic (meaning they looked and acted like humans) and often manifested parts of nature (such as Zeus, the god of thunder) or society (Hera, the goddess of marriage).

30. **Philosopher King:** Plato's idea of the ideal ruler for his ideal state. Only philosophers may truly understand justice, and so must apply their understanding to rule.

31. ***Polis* (plural *polites*):** term in ancient Greece for city-state. The *polis* was usually ruled by their citizen bodies (that is, organized according to a specific

constitution).*

32. **Political Naturalism:** theory that human political associations are natural rather than (as it is commonly believed) people living "away" from nature.

33. **Polity:** rule by the citizens; for Aristotle, the best form of constitutional government.

34. **Populist:** a person who seeks to appeal to many masses of people, often used negatively.

35. **Practical Reason (*phronesis*):** connection of reasoning to action (instead of pure theorizing, which is unconnected to action).

    Philosophers who emphasize *phronesis* will think of what is right *in the real world*; philosophers who do not will theorize purely in the abstract.

36. **Pre-Socratic Philosophy:** schools of philosophical thought in or near Ancient Greece that were not influenced by Socrates. They focused on explaining the substance of the natural world.

37. **Rhetoric:** the art and theory of persuasive language, either written or spoken.

38. **Scholasticism:** school of thought that originated in medieval universities and religious institutions. This method examined sources of wisdom (philosophers, theologians, the Bible, and so on) to uncover the knowledge they offered.

39. **Teleology:** an understanding of historical events, actions, or objects founded on the idea that they exist for their purpose rather than their cause or the forces that brought them into being.

40. **Theology:** systematic, academic study of religious principles.

41. **Tyranny:** rule by a single individual, acting in his own interests, at the expense of a stable society.

42. **United Nations Development Program (UNDP):** formed in 1965, an executive board in the United Nations System dedicated to reducing poverty with a number of broader human-development goals, including the promotion

global health, literacy, and democracy.

43. **Utopia:** a paradise or otherwise perfect situation—usually an impossibly perfect place.

44. **Virtue Ethics:** approach to ethics that emphasizes how one acts, as opposed to the rules one follows ("deontology") or the consequences of one's actions ("consequentialism").

45. **Virtue:** in the way Aristotle uses the term, "virtue" refers to excellence of character and proper management of one's impulses. (Eating moderately is virtuous, for example, because it requires the correct regulation of one's body.)

46. **Washington Consensus:** term coined by the economist John Williamson* to describe 10 policy prescriptions common to a reform package imposed on developing countries by financial institutions based in Washington DC and promoted by the American government. The policies emphasize macroeconomic stabilization, economic liberalization, and deficit reduction.

47. **Zoology:** scientific study of animals.

PEOPLE MENTIONED IN THE TEXT

1. **Alexander III of Macedon (commonly 'the Great') (356 – 323 B.C.E.)** was king of Macedonia who built on his father's conquests in Europe, expanding the empire through Africa and Asia before his death in Babylon.

2. **Andronicus of Rhodes (c. 60 B.C.E.)** was head of the Lyceum after Aristotle. He published a new edition of Aristotle's work, as well as commentaries on *Physics*, *Ethics*, and *Categories*.

3. **Gertrude Elizabeth Margaret (G. E. M.) Anscombe (1919 – 2001)** was a British philosopher, born in Ireland. Her work on virtue ethics, especially "Modern Moral Philosophy," is considered foundational for the discipline.

4. **St.Thomas Aquinas (1225 – 74)** was an Italian intellectual and saint who advocated "natural theology," which attempts to prove the existence of God by reasoning from nature.

5. **Ryan Balot** is a political philosopher at the University of Toronto in Canada. He is interested in how ancient philosophy can inform modern democracy.

6. **Ernest Barker (1874 – 1960)** was an English academic, primarily concerned with ancient political thought. His reinterpretation of classical philosophy for a modern context has made him one of the most important British thinkers in this vein of the twentieth century.

7. **Edmund Burke (1729 – 97)** was Irish statesman and political thinker who spent most of his career as a parliamentarian in England. He wrote on many topics, including a famously critical response to the French Revolution.

8. **J. H. Burns** was a Scottish philosopher of the history of ideas who spent most of his career at University College London. He focused on a range of topics, from medieval political philosophy to procedural issues in democracies.

9. **Paul Cartledge (b. 1947)** is a British historian who specializes in Greek culture. He is especially expert in the history and culture of ancient Sparta.

10. **Thomas Case (1844 – 1925)** was a British academic, and fellow of Magdalen College Oxford in moral philosophy.

11. **David Clark** is a lecturer in development studies at the University of Cambridge, specializing in notions of human development and cultural issues.

12. **Pierre Destrée** is a professor of ancient history and philosophy at the University of Louvain in Belgium. He specializes in Plato and Aristotle.

13. **Stephen Everson** is a lecturer in philosophy of mind at the University of York in the United Kingdom.

14. **Jill Frank** is an academic at the University of South Carolina in the United States. She specializes in classical political theory.

15. **Dorothea Frede (b. 1941)** is a professor of philosophy at the University of California, Berkeley. She is a notable commentator on Aristotle's *Ethics*.

16. **Thomas Hobbes (1588 – 1679)** was an English political philosopher. He is famous for his argument that political order is artificial, and that life in nature is "poor, nasty, brutish, and short."

17. **Werner Jaeger (1888 – 1961)** was a German classicist famous for linking the thought of Plato and Aristotle. He wrote that Aristotle is the practical application of Plato.

18. **David C. Lindberg (1935 – 2015)** was an American philosopher of science, especially the history of science in the medieval and renaissance worlds. In 1999, he received the Sarton Medal (the highest award) from the History of Science Society.

19. **Anthony Arthur (A.A.) Long (b. 1937)** is a British classical scholar at the University of California at Berkeley.

20. **Carnes Lord (b. 1944)** is a professor of strategic leadership at the US Naval War College. He is interested in different approaches to political authority throughout history.

21. **Niccolò Machiavelli (1469 – 1527)** was an Italian diplomat (from Florence), political thinker, and statesman. His work *The Prince* is considered to the first work of modern political theory.

22. **Margaret Marshall (b. 1944)** is a South African-born lawyer and judge. She served as the first woman on the Massachusetts Supreme Judicial Court.

23. **Fred D. Miller, Jr.** is an emeritus professor of philosophy at Bowling Green University who specializes in Aristotle.

24. **Martha Nussbaum (b. 1947)** is an American philosopher who specializes in virtue ethics and is one of the major figures in the renewed twentieth century interest in Aristotle. She is especially interested in including feminism in virtue ethics and development.

25. **Stefano Perfetti** is a professor of medieval and ancient history at the University of Pisa, specializing in the impact of Aristotle.

26. **Petrarch (Francisco Petrarca) (1304 – 74)** was an Italian scholar and poet. He is partially responsible for finding and popularizing Cicero's ancient work throughout Renaissance Europe.

27. **Philip II of Macedon (382 – 336 B.C.E.)** was the king of Macedonia (a region to the north of present-day Greece) and led the Macedonian conquest of Greece. He was assassinated after he united much of Greece and began invading Persia.

28. **Plato (428 – 348 B.C.E.)** was an ancient Greek philosopher and perhaps the most important philosopher in Western history. His philosophy spanned many issues—from justice, to love, to the metaphysical—and defined the approach of all who followed him for centuries.

29. **Michael Sandel (b. 1953)** is an American political philosopher. He is most famous as a theorist of justice and community.

30. **Malcolm Schofield** is a professor of classics at the University of Cambridge, specializing in ancient political thought.

31. **Amartya Sen (b. 1933)** is an Indian Economist and Nobel laureate. (He was awarded the Nobel Prize in 1998 for his work on welfare economics). He teaches at the Universities of Cambridge and Oxford, as well as Harvard

University.

32. **Socrates (470 – 399 B.C.E.)** was an ancient Greek philosopher. He never published work of his own, but those around him, especially Plato, widely reported on his ideas. His work laid the foundations of Western philosophy.

33. **Leo Strauss (1899 – 1973)** was a German American political philosopher, specializing in the history of classical philosophy. He is especially prominent among conservative thinkers, trying to extract timeless wisdom from "great books."

34. **Theophrastus (371 – 287 B.C.E.)** was the successor to Aristotle as head of the Lyceum. He is most famous for his work on classifying plants.

35. **William of Moerbeke (1215/35 – 1286)** was a Flemish medieval translator and philosopher, especially well known for translating medical and scientific texts into Latin (a language most educated people spoke at the time) from Greek (a language fewer people spoke).

36. **John Williamson (b. 1937)** is an English economist and international statesman famous for coining the term "Washington Consensus" to describe the pro-free market policy mix promoted by international financial institutions in the 1980s. He has worked with the United Nations, World Bank, and International Monetary Fund in advisory capacities.

37. **Xenophanes (570 – 475 B.C.E.)** was a pre-Socratic Greek philosopher and satirist. He was famously critical of closely held Greek beliefs, including reverence for the gods and athletic conquest.

WORKS CITED

1. Anscombe, G.E.M. "Modern Moral Philosophy." *Philosophy* 33, No. 124 (1958): 1 – 19.

2. Aquinas, St. Thomas. *Commentary on Aristotle's Politics*, translated by Richard J. Regan. Indianapolis: Hackett, 2007.

3. _____, *Summa Theologica*, (Mobilereference: 2010).

4. Aristotle, *History of the Animals*. Adelaide: University of Adelaide. ebook. https://ebooks.adelaide.edu.au/a/aristotle/history/book1.html.

5. _____. *Physics*. Translated by Robin Waterfield. Oxford: Oxford World's Classics, 2008.

6. _____. "Nicomachean Ethics: Book X, Chapter 9" in *The Politics and The Constitution of Athens*, edited by Stephen Everson of *Cambridge Texts in the History of Political Thought*, series editors Raymond Geuss and Quentin Skinner. Cambridge: Cambridge University Press, 1996.

7. _____. *Poetics*. Translated by Richard Janko. Indianapolis: Hackett Publishing, 1987.

8. _____. *Politics* in *The Politics and The Constitution of Athens*, edited by Stephen Everson of *Cambridge Texts in the History of Political Thought*, series editors Raymond Geuss and Quentin Skinner. Cambridge: Cambridge University Press, 1996.

9. Balot, Ryan. *Greek Political Thought*. Oxford: Blackwell, 2006.

10. Barker, Sir Ernest. *The Political Thought of Plato and Aristotle*. New York: Dover Publications, 1959.

11. Blackson, Thomas. *Ancient Greek Philosophy*. Chichester: Wiley-Blackwell, 2011.

12. Burke, Edmund. *Reflections on the Revolution in France*. New Haven: Yale University Press, 2003.

13. J.H. Burns. "Introduction: Politics, Institutions, and Ideas," in *The Cambridge History of Medieval Political Thought*. Cambridge: Cambridge University Press, 1988.

14. Cartledge, Paul. "Greek Political Thought: The Historical Context." In *The Cambridge History of Greek and Roman Political Thought*, edited by Christopher Rowe et al. Cambridge: Cambridge University Press, 2000.

15. Case, Thomas. "Aristotle." In *Aristotle's Philosophical Development: Problems*

and *Prospects*, edited by William Robert Wians. London: Rowman and Littlefield, 1990.

16. Clark, David. *Visions of Development: A Study of Human Values*. Cheltenham: Edward Elgar, 2002.

17. _____, "Capability Approach." In *The Elgar Companion to Development Studies*, edited by David Clark. Cheltenham: Edward Elgar Publishing Limited, 2006.

18. Destrée, Pierre. "Education, Leisure and Politics." In *The Cambridge Companion to* Aristotle's *Politics*, edited by Marguerite Deslauriers and Pierre Destrée. Cambridge and New York: Cambridge University Press, 2013.

19. Everson, Stephen, "Introduction." *The Politics and The Constitution of Athens*, edited by Stephen Everson. In *Cambridge Texts in the History of Political Thought*, series editors Raymond Geuss and Quentin Skinner. Cambridge: Cambridge University Press, 1996.

20. Frank, Jill. *A Democracy of Distinction: Aristotle and the Work of Politics*. Chicago: University of Chicago Press, 2005.

21. Frede, Dorothea. "The Political Character of Aristotle's Ethics." In *The Cambridge Companion to Aristotle's Politics*. Cambridge: Cambridge University Press, 2013.

22. Graham, Daniel. *Aristotle's Two Systems*. Oxford: Oxford University Press, 1990.

23. Hobbes, Thomas. *Leviathan*. Edited by J.C.A. Gaskin. Oxford: Oxford University Press, 1998.

24. Hursthouse, Rosalind. *On Virtue Ethics*. Oxford: Oxford University Press, 1999.

25. Jaeger, Werner. *Aristotle: Fundamentals of the History of His Development*.

26. Translated by Richard Robinson. Oxford: Oxford University Press, 1948.

27. Kleinhenz, Christopher. *Medieval Italy: An Encyclopedia Volume I A-K*. Oxford: Routledge, 2004.

28. Lindberg, David C. *The Beginnings of Western Science: The European Scientific Tradition in Philosophical, Religious, and Institutional Context, Prehistory to AD 1450*. Chicago: University of Chicago, 2008.

29. Long, A.A. "The Scope of Early Greek Philosophy." In *The Cambridge Companion to Early Greek Philosophy*. Cambridge: Cambridge University Press,

1999.

30. Lord, Carnes. "The Character and Composition of Aristotle's *Politics*." *Political Theory* 9, No. 4 (1981): 459 – 478.

31. Lynch, John Patrick. *Aristotle's School: A Study of a Greek Educational Institution*. Berkeley: University of California Press, 1972.

32. Machiavelli, Niccolò. *The Prince*. Edited by Quentin Skinner and Russell Price. Cambridge: Cambridge University Press, 1988.

33. Martin, Conor. "Some Medieval Commentaries on Aristotle's *Politics*." *History* 36 (1951) 126 – 127: 29 – 44.

34. Miller, Fred D. "Aristotelian Statecraft and Modern Politics." In *Aristotle's Politics Today*. Edited by Lenn E. Goodman and Robert B. Talisse. Albany: State University of New York Press, 2008.

35. Natali, Carlo. *Aristotle: His Life and School*. Princeton: Princeton University Press, 2013.

36. Nussbaum, Martha. "Non-Relative Virtues: An Aristotelian Approach." *Midwest Studies in Philosophy 13*. No. 1 (1988): 32 – 53.

37. _____. *Women and Human Development: The Capabilities Approach*. Cambridge: Cambridge University Press, 2000.

38. Perfetti, Stefano. *Aristotle's Zoology and its Renaissance Commentators*. Leuven: Leuven University Press, 2000.

39. Plato, *The Republic*. Edited by G.R.F. Ferrarri. In *Cambridge Texts in the History of Political Thought*, series editors Raymond Geuss and Quentin Skinner.

40. Cambridge: Cambridge University Press, 2003.

41. _____. Plato, *Gorgias*, translated by Robin Waterfield. Oxford: Oxford World's Classics, 1995.

42. Sacks, David. "Xenophanes." In *A Dictionary of the Ancient Greek World*. Oxford: Oxford University Press, 1995.

43. Sandel, Michael. "Justice: What's the Right Thing to Do?" *Boston University Law Review* 91 (2011): 1301 – 1569.

44. Schofield, Malcolm. "Aristotle: An Introduction," In *The Cambridge History of Greek and Roman Political Thought*, edited by Christopher Rowe et al. Cambridge: Cambridge University Press, 2000.

45. _____. "Ideology and Philosophy in Aristotle's Theory of Slavery." In *Aristotle's Politics: Critical Essays*, edited by Richard Kraut and Steven Skultety. Lanham: Rowman and Littlefield, 2005.
46. Sen, Amartya. *Development as Freedom*. New York: Alfred A. Knopf, 1999.
47. Strauss, Leo *The City and Man*. Chicago: University of Chicago Press, 1964.
48. United Nations, "Human Development Reports." Accessed Feb 25, 2014, http: // hdr.undp.org/en/statistics/hdi.
49. Williamson, John. "What Washington means by Policy Reform," in *Latin American Adjustment: How Much Has Happened?* edited by John Williamson. Washington: Institute for International Economics, March 1990. Accessed July 19, 2015, http: //www.iie.com/publications/papers/paper.cfm?researchid=486.

原书作者简介

亚里士多德于公元前384年出生在今马其顿，17岁前往希腊雅典，师从欧洲哲学奠基人之一柏拉图，在著名的柏拉图学园学习哲学。公元前347年柏拉图去世后，亚里士多德回到马其顿，为年轻的亚历山大大帝担任导师，后于公元前335年重返雅典，自办吕克昂学园。政治动荡迫使亚里士多德于公元前322年再度离开雅典，不久便在埃维亚岛去世。

本书作者简介

凯瑟琳·贝里斯福德在埃克塞特大学进行政治理论博士论文研究。
赖利·奎因获伦敦政治经济学院、牛津大学政治学及国际关系硕士学位。

世界名著中的批判性思维

世界思想宝库钥匙丛书致力于深入浅出地阐释全世界著名思想家的观点，不论是谁、在何处都能了解到，从而推进批判性思维发展。

世界思想宝库钥匙丛书与世界顶尖大学的一流学者合作，为一系列学科中最有影响的著作推出新的分析文本，介绍其观点和影响。在这一不断扩展的系列中，每种选入的著作都代表了历经时间考验的思想典范。通过为这些著作提供必要背景、揭示原作者的学术渊源以及说明这些著作所产生的影响，本系列图书希望让读者以新视角看待这些划时代的经典之作。读者应学会思考、运用并挑战这些著作中的观点，而不是简单接受它们。

ABOUT THE AUTHOR OF THE ORIGINAL WORK

Aristotle was born in 384 B.C.E. in what is present-day Macedonia. At the age of 17 he moved to Athens in Greece to begin an education in philosophy under Plato, one of the founders of European philosophy, at his renowned Academy. On Plato's death in 347 B.C.E., Aristotle moved back to Macedonia to tutor the young Alexander the Great. But in 335 B.C.E. he returned to Athens and established his own school, the Lyceum.

Political unrest forced Aristotle to leave Athens again in 322 B.C.E., and he died shortly afterwards on the island of Euboea.

ABOUT THE AUTHOR OF THE ANALYSIS

Katherine Berrisford is researching a PhD thesis in political theory at the University of Exeter.

Riley Quinn holds master's degrees in politics and international relations from both LSE and the University of Oxford.

ABOUT MACAT
GREAT WORKS FOR CRITICAL THINKING

Macat is focused on making the ideas of the world's great thinkers accessible and comprehensible to everybody, everywhere, in ways that promote the development of enhanced critical thinking skills.

It works with leading academics from the world's top universities to produce new analyses that focus on the ideas and the impact of the most influential works ever written across a wide variety of academic disciplines. Each of the works that sit at the heart of its growing library is an enduring example of great thinking. But by setting them in context — and looking at the influences that shaped their authors, as well as the responses they provoked — Macat encourages readers to look at these classics and game-changers with fresh eyes. Readers learn to think, engage and challenge their ideas, rather than simply accepting them.

批判性思维与《政治学》

首要批判性思维技巧：解决问题
次要批判性思维技巧：评估

亚里士多德是历史上最著名的思想家之一，这很大程度上归功于其敏锐的批判性思维技巧。《政治学》被视作西方政治传统的奠基著作之一，专注于解决问题，尤其是提出并评估其他可能性。

在《政治学》中，亚里士多德的目的是确定社会的最佳组织方式。他依次研究了不同类型的组织形式，即君主政体、寡头政体和由多数人统治的共和政体，并分别作出评价。而他比先贤们更进一步。他的结论是贵族政体更为可取，因为这意味着占统治地位的公民有能力代表整个社会作出决策，此外他还将解决方案进一步校验，提出建设性问题，以便在各方案间作出合理决策。

《政治学》的研究方法具有开创性。和之前思想家们不同，亚里士多德所有的观点都基于对现实世界的评估。他最终认为，自利的问题意味着采取混合政体最有可能实现幸福。该政体是以精心制定的法律为基础，目的是在民众和精英之间实现权力平衡。这一结论牢固建立在细心评估的基础上（远不只是评判论点的充分性），是解决问题高超技巧的成果。

CRITICAL THINKING AND *POLITICS*

- Primary critical thinking skill: PROBLEM-SOLVING
- Secondary critical thinking skill: EVALUATION

Aristotle remains one of the most celebrated thinkers of all time in large part thanks to his incisive critical thinking skills. In *Politics*, which can be considered one of the foundational books of the western political tradition, the focus is on problem-solving, and particularly on the generation and evaluation of alternative possibilities.

Aristotle's aim, in *Politics*, is to determine how best to organize a society. He looks in turn at several different type of organization—kingship, oligarchy and the polity, or rule in the hands of many—and evaluates the arguments for each in turn. But he takes the exercise further than his predecessors had done. Having concluded that rule by the aristocracy would be preferable, since it would mean rule by citizens capable of taking decisions on behalf of the society as a whole, Aristotle subjects his solution to a further checking process, asking productive questions in order to make a sound decision between alternatives.

Politics was ground-breaking in its approach. Unlike previous thinkers, Aristotle based all his ideas on a practical assessment of how they would play out in the real world. Ultimately, Aristotle argues, the problem of self-interest means that the adoption of a mixed constitution — one based on carefully considered laws which aims at a balance of power between the people and the elite — is most likely to bring eudaemonia (happiness). It's a conclusion firmly based on careful evaluation (not least the process of judging the adequacy of arguments) and the product of outstanding problem-solving skills.

世界思想宝库钥匙丛书简介

世界思想宝库钥匙丛书致力于为一系列在各领域产生重大影响的人文社科类经典著作提供独特的学术探讨。每一本读物都不仅仅是原经典著作的内容摘要,而是介绍并深入研究原经典著作的学术渊源、主要观点和历史影响。这一丛书的目的是提供一套学习资料,以促进读者掌握批判性思维,从而更全面、深刻地去理解重要思想。

每一本读物分为3个部分:学术渊源、学术思想和学术影响,每个部分下有4个小节。这些章节旨在从各个方面研究原经典著作及其反响。

由于独特的体例,每一本读物不但易于阅读,而且另有一项优点:所有读物的编排体例相同,读者在进行某个知识层面的调查或研究时可交叉参阅多本该丛书中的相关读物,从而开启跨领域研究的路径。

为了方便阅读,每本读物最后还列出了术语表和人名表(在书中则以星号*标记),此外还有参考文献。

世界思想宝库钥匙丛书与剑桥大学合作,理清了批判性思维的要点,即如何通过6种技能来进行有效思考。其中3种技能让我们能够理解问题,另3种技能让我们有能力解决问题。这6种技能合称为"批判性思维PACIER模式",它们是:

分析:了解如何建立一个观点;
评估:研究一个观点的优点和缺点;
阐释:对意义所产生的问题加以理解;
创造性思维:提出新的见解,发现新的联系;
解决问题:提出切实有效的解决办法;
理性化思维:创建有说服力的观点。

了解更多信息,请浏览www.macat.com。

THE MACAT LIBRARY

The Macat Library is a series of unique academic explorations of seminal works in the humanities and social sciences — books and papers that have had a significant and widely recognised impact on their disciplines. It has been created to serve as much more than just a summary of what lies between the covers of a great book. It illuminates and explores the influences on, ideas of, and impact of that book. Our goal is to offer a learning resource that encourages critical thinking and fosters a better, deeper understanding of important ideas.

Each publication is divided into three Sections: Influences, Ideas, and Impact. Each Section has four Modules. These explore every important facet of the work, and the responses to it.

This Section-Module structure makes a Macat Library book easy to use, but it has another important feature. Because each Macat book is written to the same format, it is possible (and encouraged!) to cross-reference multiple Macat books along the same lines of inquiry or research. This allows the reader to open up interesting interdisciplinary pathways.

To further aid your reading, lists of glossary terms and people mentioned are included at the end of this book (these are indicated by an asterisk [*] throughout) — as well as a list of works cited.

Macat has worked with the University of Cambridge to identify the elements of critical thinking and understand the ways in which six different skills combine to enable effective thinking.

Three allow us to fully understand a problem; three more give us the tools to solve it. Together, these six skills make up the PACIER model of critical thinking. They are:

ANALYSIS — understanding how an argument is built
EVALUATION — exploring the strengths and weaknesses of an argument
INTERPRETATION — understanding issues of meaning
CREATIVE THINKING — coming up with new ideas and fresh connections
PROBLEM-SOLVING — producing strong solutions
REASONING — creating strong arguments

To find out more, visit WWW.MACAT.COM.

"世界思想宝库钥匙丛书提供了独一无二的跨学科学习和研究工具。它介绍那些革新了各自学科研究的经典著作，还邀请全世界一流专家和教育机构进行严谨的分析，为每位读者打开世界顶级教育的大门。"

——安德烈亚斯·施莱歇尔，
经济合作与发展组织教育与技能司司长

"世界思想宝库钥匙丛书直面大学教育的巨大挑战……他们组建了一支精干而活跃的学者队伍，来推出在研究广度上颇具新意的教学材料。"

——布罗尔斯教授、勋爵，剑桥大学前校长

"世界思想宝库钥匙丛书的愿景令人赞叹。它通过分析和阐释那些曾深刻影响人类思想以及社会、经济发展的经典文本，提供了新的学习方法。它推动批判性思维，这对于任何社会和经济体来说都是至关重要的。这就是未来的学习方法。"

——查尔斯·克拉克阁下，英国前教育大臣

"对于那些影响了各自领域的著作，世界思想宝库钥匙丛书能让人们立即了解到围绕那些著作展开的评论性言论，这让该系列图书成为在这些领域从事研究的师生们不可或缺的资源。"

——威廉·特朗佐教授，加利福尼亚大学圣地亚哥分校

"Macat offers an amazing first-of-its-kind tool for interdisciplinary learning and research. Its focus on works that transformed their disciplines and its rigorous approach, drawing on the world's leading experts and educational institutions, opens up a world-class education to anyone."

—— Andreas Schleicher, Director for Education and Skills, Organisation for Economic Co-operation and Development

"Macat is taking on some of the major challenges in university education... They have drawn together a strong team of active academics who are producing teaching materials that are novel in the breadth of their approach."

—— Prof Lord Broers, former Vice-Chancellor of the University of Cambridge

"The Macat vision is exceptionally exciting. It focuses upon new modes of learning which analyse and explain seminal texts which have profoundly influenced world thinking and so social and economic development. It promotes the kind of critical thinking which is essential for any society and economy. This is the learning of the future."

—— Rt Hon Charles Clarke, former UK Secretary of State for Education

"The Macat analyses provide immediate access to the critical conversation surrounding the books that have shaped their respective discipline, which will make them an invaluable resource to all of those, students and teachers, working in the field."

—— Prof William Tronzo, University of California at San Diego

The Macat Libary
世界思想宝库钥匙丛书

TITLE	中文书名	类别
An Analysis of Arjun Appadurai's *Modernity at Large: Cultural Dimensions of Globalisation*	解析阿尔君·阿帕杜莱《消失的现代性：全球化的文化维度》	人类学
An Analysis of Claude Lévi-Strauss's *Structural Anthropology*	解析克劳德·列维-斯特劳斯《结构人类学》	人类学
An Analysis of Marcel Mauss's *The Gift*	解析马塞尔·莫斯《礼物》	人类学
An Analysis of Jared M. Diamond's *Guns, Germs, and Steel: The Fate of Human Societies*	解析贾雷德·戴蒙德《枪炮、病菌与钢铁：人类社会的命运》	人类学
An Analysis of Clifford Geertz's *The Interpretation of Cultures*	解析克利福德·格尔茨《文化的解释》	人类学
An Analysis of Philippe Ariès's *Centuries of Childhood: A Social History of Family Life*	解析菲力浦·阿利埃斯《儿童的世纪：旧制度下的儿童和家庭生活》	人类学
An Analysis of W. Chan Kim & Renée Mauborgne's *Blue Ocean Strategy*	解析金伟灿/勒妮·莫博涅《蓝海战略》	商业
An Analysis of John P. Kotter's *Leading Change*	解析约翰·P.科特《领导变革》	商业
An Analysis of Michael E. Porter's *Competitive Strategy: Creating and Sustaining Superior Performance*	解析迈克尔·E.波特《竞争战略：分析产业和竞争对手的技术》	商业
An Analysis of Jean Lave & Etienne Wenger's *Situated Learning: Legitimate Peripheral Participation*	解析琼·莱夫/艾蒂纳·温格《情境学习：合法的边缘性参与》	商业
An Analysis of Douglas McGregor's *The Human Side of Enterprise*	解析道格拉斯·麦格雷戈《企业的人性面》	商业
An Analysis of Milton Friedman's *Capitalism and Freedom*	解析米尔顿·弗里德曼《资本主义与自由》	商业
An Analysis of Ludwig von Mises's *The Theory of Money and Credit*	解析路德维希·冯·米塞斯《货币和信用理论》	经济学
An Analysis of Adam Smith's *The Wealth of Nations*	解析亚当·斯密《国富论》	经济学
An Analysis of Thomas Piketty's *Capital in the Twenty-First Century*	解析托马斯·皮凯蒂《21世纪资本论》	经济学
An Analysis of Nassim Nicholas Taleb's *The Black Swan: The Impact of the Highly Improbable*	解析纳西姆·尼古拉斯·塔勒布《黑天鹅：如何应对不可预知的未来》	经济学
An Analysis of Ha-Joon Chang's *Kicking Away the Ladder*	解析张夏准《富国陷阱：发达国家为何踢开梯子》	经济学
An Analysis of Thomas Robert Malthus's *An Essay on the Principle of Population*	解析托马斯·马尔萨斯《人口论》	经济学

An Analysis of John Maynard Keynes's *The General Theory of Employment, Interest and Money*	解析约翰·梅纳德·凯恩斯《就业、利息和货币通论》	经济学
An Analysis of Milton Friedman's *The Role of Monetary Policy*	解析米尔顿·弗里德曼《货币政策的作用》	经济学
An Analysis of Burton G. Malkiel's *A Random Walk Down Wall Street*	解析伯顿·G.马尔基尔《漫步华尔街》	经济学
An Analysis of Friedrich A. Hayek's *The Road to Serfdom*	解析弗里德里希·A.哈耶克《通往奴役之路》	经济学
An Analysis of Charles P. Kindleberger's *Manias, Panics, and Crashes: A History of Financial Crises*	解析查尔斯·P.金德尔伯格《疯狂、惊恐和崩溃：金融危机史》	经济学
An Analysis of Amartya Sen's *Development as Freedom*	解析阿玛蒂亚·森《以自由看待发展》	经济学
An Analysis of Rachel Carson's *Silent Spring*	解析蕾切尔·卡森《寂静的春天》	地理学
An Analysis of Charles Darwin's *On the Origin of Species: by Means of Natural Selection, or The Preservation of Favoured Races in the Struggle for Life*	解析查尔斯·达尔文《物种起源》	地理学
An Analysis of World Commission on Environment and Development's *The Brundtland Report, Our Common Future*	解析世界环境与发展委员会《布伦特兰报告：我们共同的未来》	地理学
An Analysis of James E. Lovelock's *Gaia: A New Look at Life on Earth*	解析詹姆斯·E.拉伍洛克《盖娅：地球生命的新视野》	地理学
An Analysis of Paul Kennedy's *The Rise and Fall of the Great Powers: Economic Change and Military Conflict from 1500—2000*	解析保罗·肯尼迪《大国的兴衰：1500—2000年的经济变革与军事冲突》	历史
An Analysis of Janet L. Abu-Lughod's *Before European Hegemony: The World System A. D. 1250—1350*	解析珍妮特·L.阿布-卢格霍德《欧洲霸权之前：1250—1350年的世界体系》	历史
An Analysis of Alfred W. Crosby's *The Columbian Exchange: Biological and Cultural Consequences of 1492*	解析艾尔弗雷德·W.克罗斯比《哥伦布大交换：1492年以后的生物影响和文化冲击》	历史
An Analysis of Tony Judt's *Postwar: A History of Europe since 1945*	解析托尼·贾德《战后欧洲史》	历史
An Analysis of Richard J. Evans's *In Defence of History*	解析理查德·J.艾文斯《捍卫历史》	历史
An Analysis of Eric Hobsbawm's *The Age of Revolution: Europe 1789–1848*	解析艾瑞克·霍布斯鲍姆《革命的年代：欧洲1789—1848年》	历史

An Analysis of Roland Barthes's *Mythologies*	解析罗兰·巴特《神话学》	文学与批判理论
An Analysis of Simon de Beauvoir's *The Second Sex*	解析西蒙娜·德·波伏娃《第二性》	文学与批判理论
An Analysis of Edward W. Said's *Orientalism*	解析爱德华·W. 萨义德《东方主义》	文学与批判理论
An Analysis of Virginia Woolf's *A Room of One's Own*	解析弗吉尼亚·伍尔芙《一间自己的房间》	文学与批判理论
An Analysis of Judith Butler's *Gender Trouble*	解析朱迪斯·巴特勒《性别麻烦》	文学与批判理论
An Analysis of Ferdinand de Saussure's *Course in General Linguistics*	解析费尔迪南·德·索绪尔《普通语言学教程》	文学与批判理论
An Analysis of Susan Sontag's *On Photography*	解析苏珊·桑塔格《论摄影》	文学与批判理论
An Analysis of Walter Benjamin's *The Work of Art in the Age of Mechanical Reproduction*	解析瓦尔特·本雅明《机械复制时代的艺术作品》	文学与批判理论
An Analysis of W.E.B. Du Bois's *The Souls of Black Folk*	解析 W.E.B. 杜博伊斯《黑人的灵魂》	文学与批判理论
An Analysis of Plato's *The Republic*	解析柏拉图《理想国》	哲学
An Analysis of Plato's *Symposium*	解析柏拉图《会饮篇》	哲学
An Analysis of Aristotle's *Metaphysics*	解析亚里士多德《形而上学》	哲学
An Analysis of Aristotle's *Nicomachean Ethics*	解析亚里士多德《尼各马可伦理学》	哲学
An Analysis of Immanuel Kant's *Critique of Pure Reason*	解析伊曼努尔·康德《纯粹理性批判》	哲学
An Analysis of Ludwig Wittgenstein's *Philosophical Investigations*	解析路德维希·维特根斯坦《哲学研究》	哲学
An Analysis of G.W.F. Hegel's *Phenomenology of Spirit*	解析 G.W.F. 黑格尔《精神现象学》	哲学
An Analysis of Baruch Spinoza's *Ethics*	解析巴鲁赫·斯宾诺莎《伦理学》	哲学
An Analysis of Hannah Arendt's *The Human Condition*	解析汉娜·阿伦特《人的境况》	哲学
An Analysis of G.E.M. Anscombe's *Modern Moral Philosophy*	解析 G.E.M. 安斯康姆《现代道德哲学》	哲学
An Analysis of David Hume's *An Enquiry Concerning Human Understanding*	解析大卫·休谟《人类理解研究》	哲学

An Analysis of Søren Kierkegaard's *Fear and Trembling*	解析索伦·克尔凯郭尔《恐惧与战栗》	哲学
An Analysis of René Descartes's *Meditations on First Philosophy*	解析勒内·笛卡尔《第一哲学沉思录》	哲学
An Analysis of Friedrich Nietzsche's *On the Genealogy of Morality*	解析弗里德里希·尼采《论道德的谱系》	哲学
An Analysis of Gilbert Ryle's *The Concept of Mind*	解析吉尔伯特·赖尔《心的概念》	哲学
An Analysis of Thomas Kuhn's *The Structure of Scientific Revolutions*	解析托马斯·库恩《科学革命的结构》	哲学
An Analysis of John Stuart Mill's *Utilitarianism*	解析约翰·斯图亚特·穆勒《功利主义》	哲学
An Analysis of Aristotle's *Politics*	解析亚里士多德《政治学》	政治学
An Analysis of Niccolò Machiavelli's *The Prince*	解析尼科洛·马基雅维利《君主论》	政治学
An Analysis of Karl Marx's *Capital*	解析卡尔·马克思《资本论》	政治学
An Analysis of Benedict Anderson's *Imagined Communities*	解析本尼迪克特·安德森《想象的共同体》	政治学
An Analysis of Samuel P. Huntington's *The Clash of Civilizations and the Remaking of World Order*	解析塞缪尔·P.亨廷顿《文明的冲突与世界秩序重建》	政治学
An Analysis of Alexis de Tocqueville's *Democracy in America*	解析阿列克西·德·托克维尔《论美国的民主》	政治学
An Analysis of J. A. Hobson's *Imperialism: A Study*	解析约·阿·霍布森《帝国主义》	政治学
An Analysis of Thomas Paine's *Common Sense*	解析托马斯·潘恩《常识》	政治学
An Analysis of John Rawls's *A Theory of Justice*	解析约翰·罗尔斯《正义论》	政治学
An Analysis of Francis Fukuyama's *The End of History and the Last Man*	解析弗朗西斯·福山《历史的终结与最后的人》	政治学
An Analysis of John Locke's *Two Treatises of Government*	解析约翰·洛克《政府论》	政治学
An Analysis of Sun Tzu's *The Art of War*	解析孙武《孙子兵法》	政治学
An Analysis of Henry Kissinger's *World Order: Reflections on the Character of Nations and the Course of History*	解析亨利·基辛格《世界秩序》	政治学
An Analysis of Jean-Jacques Rousseau's *The Social Contract*	解析让-雅克·卢梭《社会契约论》	政治学

An Analysis of Odd Arne Westad's *The Global Cold War: Third World Interventions and the Making of Our Times*	解析文安立《全球冷战：美苏对第三世界的干涉与当代世界的形成》	政治学
An Analysis of Sigmund Freud's *The Interpretation of Dreams*	解析西格蒙德·弗洛伊德《梦的解析》	心理学
An Analysis of William James' *The Principles of Psychology*	解析威廉·詹姆斯《心理学原理》	心理学
An Analysis of Philip Zimbardo's *The Lucifer Effect*	解析菲利普·津巴多《路西法效应》	心理学
An Analysis of Leon Festinger's *A Theory of Cognitive Dissonance*	解析利昂·费斯汀格《认知失调论》	心理学
An Analysis of Richard H. Thaler & Cass R. Sunstein's *Nudge: Improving Decisions about Health, Wealth, and Happiness*	解析理查德·H. 泰勒／卡斯·R. 桑斯坦《助推：如何做出有关健康、财富和幸福的更优决策》	心理学
An Analysis of Gordon Allport's *The Nature of Prejudice*	解析高尔登·奥尔波特《偏见的本质》	心理学
An Analysis of Steven Pinker's *The Better Angels of Our Nature: Why Violence Has Declined*	解析斯蒂芬·平克《人性中的善良天使：暴力为什么会减少》	心理学
An Analysis of Stanley Milgram's *Obedience to Authority*	解析斯坦利·米尔格拉姆《对权威的服从》	心理学
An Analysis of Betty Friedan's *The Feminine Mystique*	解析贝蒂·弗里丹《女性的奥秘》	心理学
An Analysis of David Riesman's *The Lonely Crowd: A Study of the Changing American Character*	解析大卫·理斯曼《孤独的人群：美国人社会性格演变之研究》	社会学
An Analysis of Franz Boas's *Race, Language and Culture*	解析弗朗兹·博厄斯《种族、语言与文化》	社会学
An Analysis of Pierre Bourdieu's *Outline of a Theory of Practice*	解析皮埃尔·布尔迪厄《实践理论大纲》	社会学
An Analysis of Max Weber's *The Protestant Ethic and the Spirit of Capitalism*	解析马克斯·韦伯《新教伦理与资本主义精神》	社会学
An Analysis of Jane Jacobs's *The Death and Life of Great American Cities*	解析简·雅各布斯《美国大城市的死与生》	社会学
An Analysis of C. Wright Mills's *The Sociological Imagination*	解析C. 赖特·米尔斯《社会学的想象力》	社会学
An Analysis of Robert E. Lucas Jr.'s *Why doesn't Capital Flow from Rich to Poor Countries?*	解析小罗伯特·E. 卢卡斯《为何资本不从富国流向穷国？》	社会学

An Analysis of Émile Durkheim's *On Suicide*	解析埃米尔·迪尔凯姆《自杀论》	社会学
An Analysis of Eric Hoffer's *The True Believer: Thoughts on the Nature of Mass Movements*	解析埃里克·霍弗《狂热分子：群众运动圣经》	社会学
An Analysis of Jared M. Diamond's *Collapse: How Societies Choose to Fail or Survive*	解析贾雷德·M.戴蒙德《大崩溃：社会如何选择兴亡》	社会学
An Analysis of Michel Foucault's *The History of Sexuality Vol. 1: The Will to Knowledge*	解析米歇尔·福柯《性史（第一卷）：求知意志》	社会学
An Analysis of Michel Foucault's *Discipline and Punish*	解析米歇尔·福柯《规训与惩罚》	社会学
An Analysis of Richard Dawkins's *The Selfish Gene*	解析理查德·道金斯《自私的基因》	社会学
An Analysis of Antonio Gramsci's *Prison Notebooks*	解析安东尼奥·葛兰西《狱中札记》	社会学
An Analysis of Augustine's *Confessions*	解析奥古斯丁《忏悔录》	神学
An Analysis of C. S. Lewis's *The Abolition of Man*	解析C.S.路易斯《人之废》	神学

图书在版编目（CIP）数据

解析亚里士多德《政治学》/凯瑟琳·贝里斯福德（Katherine Berrisford），赖利·奎因（Riley Quinn）著；杨乐译. —上海：上海外语教育出版社，2019
（世界思想宝库钥匙丛书）
ISBN 978-7-5446-5793-8

Ⅰ. ①解… Ⅱ. ①凯… ②赖… ③杨… Ⅲ. ①亚里士多德—政治哲学—研究 Ⅳ. ①B502.233 ②D0

中国版本图书馆CIP数据核字（2019）第053156号

This Chinese-English bilingual edition of *An Analysis of Aristotle's* Politics is published by arrangement with Macat International Limited.
Licensed for sale throughout the world.
本书汉英双语版由Macat国际有限公司授权上海外语教育出版社有限公司出版。
供在全世界范围内发行、销售。

图字：09-2018-549

出版发行：**上海外语教育出版社**
（上海外国语大学内） 邮编：200083
电　　话：021-65425300（总机）
电子邮箱：bookinfo@sflep.com.cn
网　　址：http://www.sflep.com
责任编辑：杨莹雪

印　　刷：上海信老印刷厂
开　　本：890×1240　1/32　印张5.5　字数112千字
版　　次：2019年8月第1版　2019年8月第1次印刷
印　　数：2 100册
书　　号：ISBN 978-7-5446-5793-8 / D
定　　价：30.00元

本版图书如有印装质量问题，可向本社调换
质量服务热线：4008-213-263　电子邮箱：editorial@sflep.com